Discovering the Spirit of the Gospels

Volume I
Matthew, Mark, Luke

Marilyn Gustin

LIGUORI
PUBLICATIONS

One Liguori Drive
Liguori, MO 63057-9999
(314) 464-2500

Imprimi Potest:
James Shea, C.SS.R.
Provincial, St. Louis Province
The Redemptorists

Imprimatur:
+ Edward J. O'Donnell, D.D.
Auxiliary Bishop, Archdiocese of St. Louis

ISBN 0-89243-681-6
Library of Congress Catalog Card Number: 94-77831

Copyright © 1994, Marilyn Gustin
Printed in the United States of America
First Edition

Cover design by Ross Sherman

CONTENTS

INTRODUCTION

This book is designed to be used. Some books, like novels, pull us from one page to another; and when we have come to the last page, we are finished with the book. I hope that you will enjoy reading *Discovering the Spirit of the Gospels,* but not stop at the last page. The book can be a basic "how-to" for your continually deepening discipleship to Jesus if you choose to use it actively.

With that in mind, here are some suggestions about how to get the most out of this book:

From start to finish, read with Bible at hand and open to the gospels. Many references mentioned here are too long to quote in full, but you will want to read them for your own best understanding. Make it easy for yourself and have the Bible ready. You may wish to put a marker at the beginning of Matthew and one at Mark and one at Luke. All but a couple of the references come from these three books.

If you like to read a book entirely through before you begin working with it, skip the questions for reflection on the first reading; but don't skip the Bible references. This is necessary for a true understanding of what is written here—and I have assumed that you will read them! You will find very little retelling of the stories or quoting of the references.

When working with the book, keep notes on the reflection questions; don't just read them through and go on. If you are serious about improving the quality of your spiritual discipleship, you will want to reflect on the questions and note your current responses. Date your responses so that a year from now you can easily see how much you have grown.

One word used often in the book may need a bit of explanation: *Synoptics*. This is a word scholars commonly use to refer to the Gospels of Matthew, Mark, and Luke. The word itself means "seeing together." It simply means that these three gospels have quite a few close similarities.

While the Synoptics have a great deal in common, they also include differences. Mark was the first gospel to be written down, probably around A.D 70. Matthew and Luke were written about twenty years after Mark, and both used Mark's material. Matthew and Luke also had other sources in common, but these have not survived for us to read. In addition, each of the three gospels includes material unique to it.

Where I have thought reading more than one version of a particular passage might interest you, I have mentioned the others or put references to them in parentheses, for example, (Matthew x:xx). Sometimes I have included the sign //, meaning parallel, indicating that a parallel or similar passage is found in that reference.

CHAPTER ONE

THE GOAL AND THE GUIDE

What was Jesus about? What were his purposes? After nearly two thousand years of Christian reflection, we have a considerable understanding of these questions. We might say, for example, that Jesus was about "redemption" or "salvation" or "forgiveness of sins." All true—but for our everyday life, how practical are they?

The answer to that question is not intended to be theoretical. Jesus' purposes were aimed toward his followers, for their benefit. He acted so that his disciples, then and now, could discover what he was and become like him. He lived close to God; he wants his followers to do the same.

No theory by itself is capable of taking anyone close to God. Not even an acceptance of correct theology will do that by itself. Jesus himself said, "Not everyone who says to me, 'Lord, Lord,' will enter the kingdom of heaven, but only the one who does the will of my Father in heaven" (Matthew 7:21).

Imagine! It is not enough to believe the right ideas about Jesus or even to call him Lord. A disciple of Jesus is urged to *follow*, which means to "take action." The action taken, when it is obedient to the teachings of Jesus, will transform that person's relationship with God and his or her whole experience of life. It is profound, spiritual transformation.

The actions involved in following Jesus take place in outward behavior. Yet we all know that actions flow from inside, from our thoughts and feelings. So the heart, the inner life of the disciple, is crucial. If we could stand before Jesus right now and ask the central question of discipleship, we would say to him, "What must I do? What must happen inside me? How must I act?"

Since we cannot ask Jesus physically, face to face, we examine the Synoptic Gospels to see what we can learn. We will find a path that Jesus laid out for his followers, a "spirituality" that will take the follower toward unity with Jesus.

The Kingdom of God

In the Synoptic Gospels, Jesus calls the goal of spiritual life the "Kingdom of God" or the "Kingdom of Heaven" or the "Reign of God." Obviously, these variations are in English. We simply don't know exactly how Jesus spoke about it, but the common term is *Kingdom*. In this book, we will call it simply the Kingdom.

The Kingdom refers to the goal that Jesus offered his disciples. In fact, teaching about the Kingdom and demonstrating its presence were the core of Jesus' activity, as recorded in the Synoptics.

If you are setting out on a trip, you usually have a notion of where you are going, a goal. Certainly if you are going to create a work of art, you have an idea what you want to make before you begin. Spiritual life is like a trip, in a way, so we want to know where we are headed. Spiritual life is also like creating a work of art because it involves changes in our own way of being. So we want a picture of what we are trying to create. The metaphor of the Kingdom taken from the Synoptic Gospels gives us a vision of our goal.

Matthew tells us that from the very first of Jesus' preaching, he taught that the Kingdom was "at hand." This announcement began Jesus' preaching and is threaded all through it (Matthew 4:17).

Matthew 4:23 and Luke 4:43 both say that Jesus traveled from town to town, preaching the Kingdom, and said "for I was sent for this purpose." In a way, it can be truly said that Jesus' whole work was to teach, demonstrate, and enable the Kingdom in his followers.

Jesus described the Kingdom in metaphors, similes, and stories. He said we could experience life in the Kingdom, and he taught us how. So we ask Jesus, "What must I be and do to live in your Kingdom?"

Jesus' first and most important understanding of the Kingdom is stated in Luke 17:20-21: "The Kingdom of God is not coming with things that can be observed; nor will they say, 'Look, here it is!' or 'There it is!' For, in fact, the kingdom of God is among you."

First, then, the coming of the Kingdom is not observable. That immediately implies that it is not a physical event or a physical place—those are both observable, aren't they? It was important for Jesus to get this straight with his first disciples, because they were expecting a physical kingdom to be established on the earth. Today, most people probably no longer expect that. If there are some who do, however, here is the gospel's response: Don't look for a physical place or institution or event. The Kingdom's arrival is not observable, not here or there. It cannot be mapped or traveled to on an interstate.

Many Christians react to the nonphysical nature of the Kingdom by concluding that it must, then, be in the afterlife. Certainly that is one dimension of the Kingdom, its most glorious aspect. Some of Jesus' words seem to refer to the afterlife. Most of his teachings about the Kingdom, however, such as the ones we just read from Luke 17:21, tell us that the Kingdom is neither a different place nor a different time. *The Kingdom of God is among you* means "now, here." Wherever you and I happen to be is the "place and time" to discover the Kingdom.

The word *among* is vital to our understanding. In its Greek form, this preposition can mean either "among" or "within, inside." Translators have to choose which English term to use. In modern times, translation committees have tended to choose "among" and to put "within" in a footnote. Older versions and modern individual translators literally seem to prefer "within."

Maybe we don't really have to choose, however. Perhaps the author of Luke's Gospel deliberately used a word that could be read both ways. If the Kingdom is among us, it means now, here, and in our relationships with one another. If the Kingdom is within us, it means that each of us has the possibility of an interior life with Jesus, with God. Both of these possibilities must be true, given the rest of Jesus' teaching in the gospels. They can't be separated. They are like two sides of one coin—without both sides, there is no coin at all.

So let us hold with the insight of the Greek and understand that the Kingdom of God is both within us (an interior life) and among us (a relational life). Let us remember that *Kingdom*, for purposes of discipleship-in-action, means neither an institution nor a physical situation. Nor does it refer primarily to a distant afterlife.

Jesus seems to have been quite fond of beginning "The Kingdom is like..." and then inventing a figurative description or story.

In Mark 4:26-32, for example, Jesus compares the Kingdom to a farmer who plants seed, which grows and ripens while the farmer is going about his life. This is the "planting" of the very beginnings of Kingdom life in the soil of our own hearts. We will not usually be able to observe it growing, but we will experience the harvest in our lives.

Likewise with the mustard seed: it is planted, tiny though it is, and then grows into a huge plant with branches large enough for birds to nest in it. Everyone knows that mustard plants are not nearly that big normally. Jesus is saying that if we plant the tiny seed of the Kingdom in our hearts, it will grow so large that it will affect every external part of our lives.

These illustrations point to both the "within us" and the "among us" of the Kingdom, don't they? It begins like a seed and then expands and expands until no part of our life is "outside" the Kingdom, but our very selves and our living are fully permeated by it. We become living expressions of the Kingdom Jesus opened to us all.

Our Guide Is Reliable

How do we know that Jesus is a reliable guide to the Kingdom? Why don't we look to someone else? The gospels address this, because in their time it was a live question. Today, we may need to recall what we so often take for granted.

Matthew tells us early on that the people who heard Jesus teach recognized a definite quality of authority in his speaking: he knew firsthand what he was talking about. At the end of the Sermon on the Mount, Matthew reports that "when Jesus had finished saying these things, the crowds were astounded at his teaching, for he taught them as one having authority…" (Matthew 7:28-29).

The gospels go even further and recall the great power of Jesus' actions. He did powerful deeds, such as healing and calming a storm and raising people from death, to demonstrate that his authority was real. The gospels suggest that Jesus can be trusted as a teacher of the Kingdom because he was strong and trustworthy in his actions.

Both points are combined in Matthew 8:5-13 (// Luke 7:1-10). The centurion recognizes Jesus' authority in the spiritual realm because he knows what it is like to live under authority in the military realm: orders given and received are obeyed. He knows that Jesus needs only to give an order and it will happen. Jesus commends the soldier's certainty, saying that this kind of awareness and trust will bring people into the Kingdom. His statement is then validated by the fact that the centurion's servant at home was healed by Jesus' authoritative order alone.

After demonstrating Jesus' power and authority in several chapters, Matthew records for us a familiar scene in 16:13-17 (// Mark 8:27-33 and Luke 9:18-22). Jesus has asked his disciples who they think he is. Peter replies, "You are the Messiah, the Son of the living God." Jesus says that is true; it is, in fact, a revelation from the heavenly Father.

Then follows the most dramatic confirmation of all, the Transfiguration of Jesus. You will find it in all three Synoptics: Matthew 17:1-8, Mark 9:2-8, and Luke 9:28-36. In Luke, the vision closes with a divine voice coming from the cloud and saying, "This is my Son, my Chosen; listen to him!" God has directed the disciples definitively to Jesus.

The Son of God lives closest to the Father's heart, does he not? If that is so, then Jesus is the best guide to living in the Kingdom of God. If we want life in the Kingdom, we attain it quickly and truly by becoming disciples of Jesus, by following this utterly reliable guide. In fact, the Kingdom belongs to Jesus Christ. He is its sovereign. So if we love Jesus, we will want to live in his Kingdom. Or if we are captivated by the idea of life in the Kingdom, we will follow Jesus.

Reflection

1. Do you act on Jesus' suggestions for finding the Kingdom to the same extent you act on, say, the directions of a
   native of a place you're visiting? Why do you act on Jesus'
   ideas? If you do not act on them, why not?
2. Who or what in your experience speaks with authority
   that you recognize directly?
3. Describe your attitude toward change. Include your feelings about self-justification, being comfortable, and your
   willingness to experiment with new actions.

CHAPTER TWO

THE FLOW BETWEEN INTERIOR LIFE AND OUTER ACTION

We already know we are affected both by what happens inside us and by what happens in outer circumstances. We have an interior life, and our actions express our outer character in the everyday world. This common experience does not change in the spiritual life. Living in the Kingdom will involve us in an ever deeper interior life with God, and our actions and circumstances will be strongly affected by our increasing closeness to the Lord.

As we grow spiritually, we begin to discover in our experience what Jesus said (and implied) over and over: what happens inside us is prior to what happens outside us. That means that our thoughts, feelings, hunches, attitudes, and innermost experiences will determine our actions. Our inner realities also create the quality of our experience in all situations.

This is why the Kingdom is understood to be within us: when we know that our foundations are interior, we recognize the Holy Spirit inside. Then, as the Spirit increasingly permeates us, our interior life expresses itself more power-fully outside. It could not be otherwise.

Jesus knew the priority of inner life. His discussions about it with his disciples challenged them. Until they learned from him, they were convinced that behavior was more important than what was inside a person.

In Matthew 15:10-20, Jesus points out this misperception in reference to the religious rules of the time. Eating with dirty hands was believed to defile the whole person and lead to ritual impurity. Ritual purity was a necessary state for per-forming any religious act and many everyday acts. On the contrary, Jesus declared, it is ugly things—ugly attitudes and thoughts—that make a person impure or unclean. Those ugly inner experiences do come out in action, however, and by this is a person made impure.

In the Sermon on the Mount, Jesus also points to the im-portance of one's inner state. In Matthew 5:21-22, Jesus re-minds his disciples of the command not to kill—an external action. He says that even anger, an internal attitude, gets one into trouble. Again in Matthew 5:27-28, he makes a similar statement about adultery. The interior attitude of lust is, for life in the Kingdom, just the same as adultery. Everyone can easily see that anger comes before murder and lust comes before adultery.

Other sayings that involve the inner and the outer sides of the Kingdom are in Matthew 13:44-46. Jesus speaks of a treasure that is "buried" in the field; that is, it is hidden within the earth. If the field is like a person, then the hiddenness refers to the inside of that person. That is where the precious treasure is to be found. The same idea is connected to the pearl: pearls are formed within the oyster. They eventually may be brought into the outside but only after being formed.

This principle is vital to understanding many of Jesus' teachings about spiritual life. Life with God assumes an inner relationship with God. Of course, that inner relationship is expressed in action, and action can, in turn, support the inner life. They are not separated, but the interior life is prior.

The Kingdom of God is first within—first in time and first in power as well. Spiritual discipleship, then, starts out hidden within the human heart. It comes later to outer expression.

The Danger of Hypocrisy

If we do not completely understand the vital importance of what is within us, we risk becoming hypocrites without even knowing it. We risk doing what looks good on the outside, even though on the inside there is quite a different quality.

Jesus got upset with very few people. Those we read the most about in the gospels are leaders who perform the right actions but whose motives and attitudes are far from God's intentions. Jesus called them hypocrites and reserved his severest criticism for them. He said they were like whitewashed tombs, looking great on the outside, but inside filled with death. (See Matthew 23:27.) In Mark 7:6, Jesus quotes the Old Testament about such people: "This people honors me with their lips, / but their hearts are far from me." It is the heart that matters to God.

It is quite possible to make our behavior fit certain rules while inside we are doing something quite different. For example, Catholics are obligated by the Church to go to Mass weekly. Many take this seriously and obey. But what are they doing in their minds and hearts while they sit in the pews? Is their presence hypocritical if they constantly wish they were somewhere else or if their thoughts keep going to yesterday or tomorrow?

It is not that rules or guidelines are wrong in themselves. Rather, the important thing is the inner state of being. The inner reality, more than the outer behavior, determines whether one lives in the Kingdom or not. Sometimes outer behavior, when chosen, can change inner reality. If that is what is intended, it's a wonderful thing. Then the inner goal is the essence of the action.

Luke 11:39-44 sums up Jesus' own concern with this issue. Let it caution us! Let us make sure that our good actions are matched and motivated by good inner attitudes and character.

In daily experience, our behavior will eventually show what our inner attitudes are. When we are caught by an unexpected situation or a sudden comment, our "true colors" show. Under stress, too, we are seldom aware enough to *force* ourselves to act in a certain way. We will be then who we really are inside.

Therefore, if we want our outside to be beautiful and our actions to be in harmony with the will of God, we will attend most carefully to what is within us. We will search actively for the inner Kingdom and learn to live in it. We will be disciples of the heart before we are doers of the Word.

Our Spiritual Relationship to Laws and Rules

If the heart's intention is what matters, then what is the function of laws or rules? If we live as close to God as Jesus did, we probably wouldn't even need to ask the question. Jesus followed many—probably most—of the rules of his Jewish religion most of the time. But he was not bound by them. Keeping the rules was certainly not his top priority.

We may not be that mature spiritually. The *intent* of rules is to support us, to help us become the people we want to be. If we use rules in this way, we will keep them as an expression of our inner love for God. Rule-keeping then will be love, not merely a matter of "shoulds"—which leads to unnecessary guilt. If we offer our obedience to God, as an act of love for God, then rules support our inner life with God.

Jesus never implied that laws and rules should be thrown away. In fact, he said that doing and teaching the laws contributed to life in the Kingdom. (See Matthew 5:18-19 and Matthew 23:2-3.) These laws are the minimum, only the basics, of life in the Kingdom. Jesus immediately urged his disciples to be better than the rule-centered Pharisees. (See Matthew 5:20.) Going a step beyond the rules, however, requires that wisdom and love be well-established in the heart.

Jesus sometimes obeyed rules when he would not have had to for the sake of other people. For example, when he was challenged about paying the temple tax (which every loyal Jew voluntarily paid), he pointed out to Peter that he was not obligated to pay it. But he would, he said, so as not to offend others. (See Matthew 17:24-27.)

These verses concerning rules suggest yet another insight: we are not *bound* by rules because we are "subjects" of God through Christ Jesus. Rules and laws do have a function for us if we obey them for the sake of relationship with Jesus. But rule-keeping will not help if it is not consistent with what is in our hearts.

Jesus expressed this relationship to rules with the metaphor of wine and wineskins. (See Matthew 9:16-17.) He implied that if we try to express new inner circumstances in the form of old rules, it won't work. Something will break. Either we will break inside or the rule will be broken outside. If we are determined to learn Kingdom living and be a full inward disciple of Jesus, it is good to keep track of our heart's realities and make sure our external actions are consistent with them.

Sometimes Jesus ignores rules if there are more important factors in the circumstances. In Mark 2:18-20, he is challenged about the failure of his disciples to fast. He replies that being with him is such a joy that, of course, they do not fast now—but they will when he is no longer so present to them. In Matthew 12:1-7, human need takes precedence over rules about the Sabbath. Healing was counted as work in those days and not allowed on the Sabbath. Jesus valued human need more than the rule and acted accordingly.

Eventually, as a person becomes very close to Jesus and really can receive Jesus' wisdom, rules become unnecessary altogether. Either they are kept automatically, simply because they are good, or they are ignored when something more important is also present. This was expressed concisely by Saint Augustine when he said, "Love, then do as you please."

The message for spiritual life, then, is this: look inside and examine your motivation for keeping the rules. If you are living a split life, you will know it as soon as you are willing to know it. If you make an occasional mistake about inner intention and rules for action, you will know what not to do the next time. If you choose to keep the rules, do so for the growth of the Kingdom within you. Then the inner qualities you desire for God's sake will be strengthened. You will be a bit closer to full discipleship because you follow the example and the guidance of the Lord.

Inner Attitude and Social Relationships

The Kingdom of God is governed by love. Two commandments are paramount in the Kingdom: love God first, and then love your neighbor as much as you love yourself. (See Mark 12:29-31.)

Jesus did not invent these commandments. He was quoting the Old Testament, namely Deuteronomy 6:4-5 and Leviticus 19:18. His original contribution was to make the Leviticus command about one's neighbor second only to the love of God. To keep these commandments is the foundation and the goal of all lesser laws.

Love is an inner quality. Our inner attitude toward God and neighbor determines everything we do, everything we say. Love is the core of life in the Kingdom. Without inner love, we may manage to be polite but not a great deal more. With love alive in our hearts—especially if our love is not dependent on the response of others—all our words and all our actions will eventually express our inner love. That is spiritual discipleship, Kingdom life.

We already know that. How deeply has it penetrated into our being? Sometimes merely knowing that love is the most important thing does not tell us concretely how to deal with society. Society seems impersonal, and its requirements sometimes seem far from questions of love. The gospels give two practical examples. What about taxes, especially if we feel that they are unjust or that the money is spent for activities we do not approve of as Christians?

Someone asked Jesus that same question. You can read about it in Mark 12:13-17. Jesus replied that disciples should give to the state what belongs to it, but give to God alone what belongs to God. Jesus does not explain further. But in the light of what we have been considering, doesn't it make sense that giving money to the state is appropriate so long as our heart is given only to God? If our heart belongs truly to God, everything else will take its rightful place. We will know that lesser things may appropriately belong to lesser realms, such as governments.

Another question that Jesus addressed has become more prevalent today than it was in Jesus' own time: what should be the stance of a disciple regarding civil suits? Luke 12:57-59 gives pretty clear advice: settle out of court as often as possible. Today one may or may not receive more money from an out-of-court settlement. But are finances the main concern of the disciple?

The long, angry, frightening, and disruptive circumstances

of a legal suit may be more important to Jesus than we imagine. Since our interior attitude is geared primarily to life in the Kingdom, we must ask where is love in civil suits?

Jesus puts a big question mark over whether a disciple should sue anyone else. What is the inner effect of a suit on a disciple? on the other party? How will this legal process and its outcome affect one's relationship with God? How can a legal process serve that relationship? These questions are raised by Jesus' comments.

If one is to be sued, then other settlement processes (like mediation) might well be sought first. Again, the purpose is to keep our heart in the peace of God, with love for all involved.

The Path of Service

Where does Mother Teresa get the stamina and persistence to keep picking people off the streets of Calcutta while administering a large religious order and traveling the world to give speeches? She is one whose passion is service. If for life in the Kingdom the inner state is prior, how does serving others relate to that?

There are do-gooders who serve for their own aggrandizement (private or public), and there are true servants who respond to needs from a deep source of compassion within their own hearts. People who set out to "do good things" for other people are inclined to let their virtue be stolen by the ego-satisfaction such actions can bring. The servant who is rooted in compassion, however, simply does not think of self, but of the one who is in need. That is Mother Teresa.

The familiar story of the Good Samaritan told by Jesus in Luke 10:29-35 is a prime example of one who simply responds. Such self-giving cannot come from pride but only from an existing inner compassion. Compassion is not quite the same as ordinary love. It is a gift from the Spirit both to the compassionate person and to the receiver of that lovely quality's expression.

The Samaritan had no external reason whatever to help the beaten man and several reasons not to do so. Acting from compassion is often like that, as we see so clearly in Mother Teresa. She, too, is rooted in God, who is purest compassion. God's compassion lives in her heart and enables her to respond and keep responding.

Another inner secret of Kingdom service is that it is humble; it may not even recognize what it has given. In Jesus' parable about the king who separated the sheep from the goats (see Matthew 25:31-45), those he commended do not even know when they have performed the service he attributed to them. He has to explain it to them.

This is evidence that service is not *essentially* an action. It is essentially an attitude of humble compassion. With such a profound and splendid inner attitude, great healing and other wonders happen in the presence of such givers.

It is hardly surprising, then, that Jesus responds to his disciples' argument about who is the greatest by saying that it is the one who serves. He goes on to say of himself that "I am among you as one who serves" (Luke 22:24-27). What do you imagine was Jesus' own motivation?

True service springs from an inner motivation of compassion. Compassion, by the example of the Lord Jesus, is the chief of all Kingdom qualities. It occurs first in the heart. Then it expresses itself in the humble and spontaneous service of others.

Clearly, Jesus did not go down a long list of all possible behaviors supportive of the Kingdom. When asked or when circumstances arose, he responded from the perspective of Kingdom values that the essential value is love for God. The second is love for other people.

Often the relationship of our inner state to a particular circumstance (like a rule or a legal matter or even another's need) does not seem concrete. When that happens, we can pray and ponder and share with others to discern what will help us live as true disciples of the Kingdom. If we ask sincerely for guidance and seek it as best we can, planning to obey it, the Lord will always direct us. He will be, as he promised, our servant, helping us into life in the Kingdom however we most need it and as deeply as we are open to it.

This is, from one viewpoint, the key to all spirituality in the Synoptic Gospels: allowing Jesus to serve us, for the Kingdom, out of his own compassion, so that we can come to intimacy with him.

Reflection

1. Consider how your attitude or deep feeling affects the quality of your experience in religious situations. Consider other types of situations, too. This demands honesty, but is very freeing when you "get it"!
2. Consider your attitude toward rule-keeping. When is love your guide in decisions about rules? When is it not your guide? Reflect also on how much guilt you feel when you choose a higher value, like love, over keeping the rules. If it seems to be too much, pray that God remove the compulsion.
3. Observe your actions and words for a few days. Are they are loving? When are they not loving? Why? What do your observations tell you about the condition of your heart?
4. Think of Jesus as your servant in your spiritual growth. Has it occurred to you that he will do whatever you want him to do to help you achieve life in the Kingdom? How does that realization feel?

CHAPTER THREE

HELPS AND OBSTACLES TO DISCIPLESHIP

Have you ever felt vaguely guilty about Jesus' call to discipleship? Many Christians do. We may feel that it is a kind of cosmic demand, something that we must agree to and must try to act on. This call makes some of us feel almost as if we were born into a huge obligation, much too big and difficult for us. We think we must answer, and it does not feel like a truly free, comfortable choice.

Yet in reading the gospels, we certainly do not receive the impression that those with whom Jesus came in contact regarded his call as a "vaguely guilty demand." People begged to be allowed to be his disciples and to travel with him on his journeys throughout Palestine. They eagerly sought his words about the Kingdom (though understanding came gradually). Those whom Jesus invited to come along with him jumped up immediately and went. Some of them donated their money to him. To be allowed to spend time, even to share a meal, with this wonderfully magnetic man was a thrill that opened exciting possibilities. It was an opportunity to be snapped up immediately, with great fascination.

Of course, those people did not know what discipleship meant at first. Everyone learned that along the way. They only knew that Jesus was a splendid person and that they wanted to be with him. They learned *how* to be with him as they listened to him and watched him and shared his life.

If we can let go of our guilty feelings about discipleship and think of it as the greatest invitation we've ever received to the most exciting adventure there is, then we have an advantage over the first disciples. We know a little bit more about *how* to be with Jesus, for we can find that in the gospels.

Jesus himself told a wonderful story about this invitation. Luke 14:15-24 gives it to us. A similar but different version is in Matthew 22:1-14.

In Luke, Jesus was at a feast in the home of a Pharisee. He was observing people there, just as they were watching him. One of the guests said, "Blessed is anyone who will eat bread in the kingdom of God." Dining at a great feast was an ancient Israelite symbol for the glories of uninterrupted life with God.

Jesus replied with the story we want to consider right now. As you read it, notice that many invitations were issued and many people didn't want to come. They were not forced. It was an invitation. No one is forced to accept an invitation. But the host was determined to have a wonderful feast, so he sent out his servants to everybody, anybody they could find— even the despised. All were invited to the feast so that "my house may be filled."

So it is with us. We are invited to Jesus' feast, to life in the Kingdom. If work or business or a human relationship is more important to us than this invitation, we say, no thanks. But if we wish to, we can go to the feast and share it with all kinds of other people who also have said yes to the invitation.

The main work of the disciples after Jesus' Ascension to the Father was to extend this invitation to everyone (Matthew 28:18-20). Jesus' glorious promise to them and to all who accepted the invitation was that he would be with them always, even as far as the end of the world.

So the invitation to discipleship is an invitation to be with Jesus, both in this lifetime and forever. If we want to accept the Lord's invitation, what comes next?

Preparation for Discipleship

The invitation to discipleship is not as simple as an invitation to our neighbor's house for supper. It is both much grander and much more challenging. It can only be called an adventure. In an adventure, we start out with a goal. We know some things that we can expect along our way, but not everything. We also have a guide who knows the terrain. But the going is not an unwelcome task. It is a great excitement! Also, an adventure is complex enough that preparation is required.

Jesus tells us to prepare. In Luke 14:28-32, Jesus recalls the examples of a person who wants to build a tower. Doesn't he first check his finances to see if he can complete it? And if a king is going into battle, doesn't he calculate his own forces against enemy forces to see if he has a chance?

Take stock, Jesus suggests.

The first thing to notice is that no one is isolated. God cares about every disciple. Jesus says, "Are not five sparrows sold for two pennies? Yet not one of them is forgotten in God's sight. But even the hairs of your head are all counted. Do not be afraid; you are of more value than many sparrows" (Luke 12:6-7 and // Matthew 10:29-31).

Furthermore, Jesus says that if the kingdom comes first for the disciple, she or he will not have to worry about the usual everyday things. They will be provided. Then, the best promise of all: "Do not be afraid, little flock, for it is your Father's good pleasure to give you the kingdom" (Luke 12:32).

Disciples can count on God to care for them, to provide what they need, and to give them the Kingdom of Jesus.

What are your own resources for discipleship? Jesus often points out that our key resource is the intensity of our desire for life in the Kingdom. Is it the most important of all your desires? Can you really put the Kingdom first? Is it more important than family obligations? (Luke 14:26 and Matthew 8:21-22). Is it more important than even your own comfort? (Luke 9:57-58). Is it more important than your own life? (Luke 9:24).

The amazing promises that go with these challenges show that, in reality, the Kingdom is more beautiful, more precious, more vital than any of our ordinary cares. No disciple can pursue the Kingdom who only thinks he or she is *supposed* to want it. But the one who genuinely does want the Kingdom and wants it very much is assured of receiving it.

Jesus is quite explicit. If the Kingdom is more important to the disciple than daily cares, those daily needs will be met (Matthew 6:31-33). If the Kingdom is more important than possessions and comforts, then inner treasures vastly more valuable will be given (Matthew 19:29, Luke 18:22, Mark 10:21). If the Kingdom is more important than one's very life, then that life will be saved and kept for all eternity (Luke 9:24).

For the fullness of interior life with Jesus in the Kingdom, it must become more important to the disciple than anything. Sometimes this very idea is frightening. People imagine that they will have to do without lots of things, maybe go far away and do some enormous job, maybe experience a lot of pain. Or they just feel as if God will let them down somehow if they are not in total control of their own living.

Here is a way to think about this that may free us from some of our hesitations. What is the key to success in *any* effort? It can be business or family, mastery of a skill, or achievement of a great dream. It doesn't matter what it is. The best success comes only when the desire is given top priority in time, in interest, in effort, in dedication.

When a person wants above all else to become a master violinist, that person chooses not to play football or do other things that put the hands at risk. That person chooses to study hard and practice a lot. That person chooses to let other fascinating possibilities go by, to fulfill the dream that possesses his or her heart. So it is also with great success in business or with a great family life. No one can do everything. No one is expected to do everything.

Those things ignored or left behind for the sake of such dreams are not experienced as terrible demands. One gives them up gladly because the dream is much more important to one's heart. That's like the glorious Kingdom to which Jesus invites us—and *that* Kingdom is inside us, free from circumstances. It can be experienced through this very life, if we want it.

Obstacles to Full Discipleship

Along the way toward every great goal, some unexpected, tough things happen. Take a mountain climber. Is every step upward going to be easy and "fun"? Hardly. Sometimes the utmost effort is required to keep putting one foot in front of the other. But if that is true for so limited a goal as a mountain summit, how much more true for the greatest adventure of all: life in the Kingdom with the Lord! Do we expect the challenge to be less for eternal things than for mundane things?

When the unexpected bad weather or the anticipated difficulties arise, what does the mountain climber do? The whole success or failure of the venture depends on the decision at such moments.

What kinds of obstacles might get in the way of discipleship coming to its full fruition in the Kingdom? And how might one begin to deal with them? Obstacles come in many forms; they seem to be tailored to the individual by the Spirit. Here we'll look at a few from the Synoptics.

One obstacle is the desire for riches and the love of riches. Jesus, you will remember, was once confronted by a wealthy young man who wanted advice. He was already doing all the right things but wanted to know what he yet lacked. Jesus invited him to get rid of his riches and to become an active disciple. But the young man loved his riches too much. He could not part with them. Jesus commented, "How hard it will be for those who have riches to enter the Kingdom!" (See Mark 10:17-27, Matthew 19:16-23, Luke 18:18-27.)

That comment is not difficult to understand. The rich often put riches above everything. They invest their time, efforts, emotions, and energies in the getting and keeping of their money and its attendant lifestyle. They are, therefore, not able to want the Kingdom enough.

However, if a person who faces this obstacle actually manages to let go of the attachment to money and lifestyle and gives away those riches, then the Kingdom would come looking for him or for her. Saint Francis of Assisi is a familiar example. Heir to a fortune, he left it all behind because he wanted Christ more. So he received Christ in all his fullness.

Another obstacle is simply distractions, not distractedness in prayer but distracted living, living that tends toward constant diversion. Every diversion takes some energy and attention away from the goal. Like the flow of water, if our energy and attention are scattered in many directions, they become shallow and spread out, sinking into the sand. If, like water, they are held within narrow banks, they get deeper and flow faster. Then, undiverted, they flow directly toward their goal.

Some kinds of distractions have already appeared as excuses for not coming to the banquet. Every life has its own *kind* of distractions. What they are is less important than how they pull the disciple away from the top priority of the Kingdom.

One way to handle distraction and diversion is to ask yourself: *Is this a step nearer to the Kingdom? Does it bring me closer to the Lord?* If it serves the direction you really want to go, do it. If not, don't do it.

Another obstacle that inevitably comes along, especially as the Kingdom begins to have noticeable effects in one's life, is the desire to be great, to have status among disciples or in the world. The first disciples met this obstacle too. You may read about it in Luke 9:46-48 (//Mark 9:33-37; Matthew 18:1-5). Jesus indicated that to handle this obstacle well, one needs to become simple and contented, like a child, in whatever circumstances one finds oneself.

The last obstacle we'll consider is fright, or lack of trust. Over and over in the gospels, Jesus says, "Do not be afraid." Fear prevents us from getting close enough to Jesus to enter the Kingdom. What happens to the frightened person is very much like what happened to Peter.

When Jesus walked across the lake toward the disciples' boat, Peter impulsively wanted to join Jesus on the water's surface. He asked permission, then hopped overboard. And he was okay, there, stepping toward Jesus. Then he noticed how awful the wind was, and he got scared. Jesus had to keep him from sinking. Fortunately, Peter had enough presence of mind to cry out to Jesus for help. (See Matthew 14:22-32.)

So it is with us. When we are afraid, we will sink. But the obstacle of fear can be removed if we call to Jesus for help with it. He will teach us to replace fear with trust. Jesus reproached Peter for his doubts, implying that if he had not been so foolish as to get frightened, he could have come all the way to Jesus on the water. If we refuse fear and learn to trust, we can go all the way to the Kingdom and always be with Jesus inside ourselves.

Toward all obstacles to the Kingdom, Jesus advises a ruthless attitude. Mark 9:43-47 reports Jesus' words. Jesus is not recommending physical self-mutilation here! He is simply saying that *nothing*, not even eyes or hands, is more important to the disciple than the Kingdom. If obstacles (or sins) get in the way, do away with them! Do away with them now! Sometimes, for our inner selves to stay close to Jesus, we have to take drastic measures against obstacles that appear in the external, ordinary world, as well as those that appear in our hearts.

Will it hurt? Probably. Does a masterful halfback hurt after hours of practice? Sure. Is it worth it? Well, what do you think?

The Community of Disciples

One of the wonderful aspects of following Jesus is that we never go alone. God is with us, Jesus is with us. And we have human companionship as well.

That's important. Few of us would arrive if we were isolated from other people of venturesome spirit like ourselves. We are called to discipleship together. The first disciples lived in a group at least part of the time. Together, they followed Jesus around, they discussed things among themselves, and they argued and tried to understand together. They were sent on their first training missions together. (See Matthew 10:1, 5-8.) And they even seem to have deserted Jesus together during his Passion and crucifixion!

Many Christians today, though certainly not all, feel alone in their dedication to life in the Kingdom, especially if they are deeply fervent and excited about it. Some church members are not particularly interested in active discipleship or interior life with God. That leaves some of the excited ones feeling alone.

In fact, no one who is excited about Jesus' invitation to the Kingdom is alone. There are always others, even though they may not sit next to you in the pew or live on your street. If we want to live in the Kingdom, we must find others who want it too. We will be eager to share with them, to hear their stories about inner growth and outer expression, and to share our own stories of obstacles overcome and hopes still ahead.

Modern disciples will search for companionship wherever it is to be found. They can often locate houses of prayer or retreat houses where residents and other visitors share their discipleship. Some disciples, in a great longing to express the inner life of the Kingdom, undertake social-justice projects. One can find company among those great servants of others. Sometimes centering prayer groups or charismatic groups include disciples. Some people find their community of determination in telephone conversations with other disciples who live miles away. Others find a sense of companionship in books that open hearts. Sometimes the most excited disciples are the quietest people—but they recognize one another by the quality of their presence.

The building of a "personal" community of disciples can be crucial to life in the Kingdom. From a community of disciples, one learns and is inspired to keep going. One is helped over obstacles. One is supported and strengthened. One gets the chance to help another on the way. The Lord often speaks to a person through another member of the community too. How often I would have missed my own next step had it not been for the sharing of another person!

Just as Jesus was wise enough to choose a group of people to follow him, so Christian spiritual life has always involved a group of others. Even hermits were not totally solitary. Today, we will not be handed a ready-made group of equally dedicated disciples. We will have to look for them and build a discipleship network. It will be indescribably rewarding. When we are together, one of our company is always the Lord, who rejoices in our presence with him.

Reflection

1. If you feel a "vague sense of guilt" about discipleship, ponder that for a moment. Then ponder your sense of adventure about life in the Kingdom. Which is stronger? Why? What do you want to change?
2. What are the distractions that turn you aside from full discipleship? After considering them clearly, decide what you want to do with them. Then do it.
3. How have you handled obstacles in the past? What obstacles still remain in you?
4. What will you do to build your own discipleship network?

CHAPTER FOUR

PRAYER

I t's a truism, yet we benefit from being reminded. No human relationship exists without two people spending time together, attending to each other and communicating. How much more this is true when a whole life is founded on a relationship with one other—God. Why do we want to be Jesus' disciples? Because we love the Lord. Why do we want to live in the Kingdom of God? Because it is increasing closeness to the Lord of all.

Have you ever been involved with another person when you felt that you took all the initiative, made all the efforts, gave all that was given, while the other one just soaked it up and returned nothing? I often think God might feel like that with us. God gives and gives. God offers and invites. God loves and loves and loves. God even creates circumstances designed to draw—or drag!—us closer to himself. How often do we happily move closer to God?

The first action we can take to bring ourselves nearer to God in our hearts is prayer. Anyone who has picked up this book surely knows that already. Are there insights from the Synoptics that can better our understanding of prayer and give us clues about how to enrich our prayer?

The gospels do not instruct us in prayer as much as we might like. Jesus must have taught his disciples much more about it. They then taught one another as new converts entered Christian life. Possibly, not much instruction in prayer appears in the gospels because the writers assumed their readers would already know that whole traditional teaching. They did not know they were writing for us, two thousand years later! Still, if we actually made a continuous effort to follow the instructions and hints we *do* have, our prayer would expand.

Let's look first at Matthew 6:5-6. Jesus objected to the habit of some who do their praying deliberately in public places so they can be seen by others. No, he says, prayer is a private matter. So when you pray, go somewhere alone. Then your relationship with God will not be muddied by your interest in other people's opinions.

Jesus intensifies this teaching by telling us to pray to the Father in secret. This can mean simply closing a door behind us. It can also refer to the innermost secret place within each of us where we are known only to ourselves and to God. We need not worry that God cannot "hear" us if only our hearts speak, without our lips. Jesus says God perceives what is in the secret place inside.

At baptism, the Holy Spirit came to dwell in us. That Spirit of Jesus is still there! So, of course, God knows what happens deep within us. In fact, "within" is altogether the best place to pray. Inner prayer is the essence of our communication with God. Inner prayer is often deeper than spoken prayer. We know without words and God hears without words. We meet God in the secret place of the heart.

Then Jesus goes on to warn against babbling. The point here is simple: God knows what we need and want before we tell him. However prayer "works," it never tells God anything he didn't know already. It is more like the kind of conversation that occurs between a husband and wife in a long and comfortable marriage. They know so much about each other! There is so much they never need to be told. Yet in their mutual love they respond to each other's words, even when they do not convey new information.

Something further occurs with God. When we open our hearts enough to ask humbly and intensely for something, we do not need to go on and on about it. The point is to be open enough to God to ask. That inner openness enables us to receive God's response.

Mark 11:22-24 offers a deeper tip. It's a bit harder to carry out than the two we have just explored. You will want to read the whole passage (Mark 11:12-14,20-25) in order to understand fully the points Jesus makes.

Jesus has just done a work that demonstrates his power. (Please, don't worry about the fig tree!) He did it to give an occasion to teach his disciples something particular. The teaching is in verses 22 and 23: trust absolutely in God, ask and *believe* and you will receive.

What kind of belief is this? It is not theological. Jesus says to "believe that you have received it." We are not always able to do that. We have a lot of doubts—about whether God hears us, about whether we really want something, about whether it is good for us, or about what the will of God is. We have doubts about whether God cares for us. Our doubts go on and on. They get very subtle. It is our habitual doubting that gets in the way of our prayer. God is ready to give.

Once I experienced a definite certainty that God would give me what I asked. For two years a dear friend had been missing a valuable bracelet of sapphires and platinum. She had been very generous to me, even letting me live with her when I was on vacation from graduate school. I wanted to do something for her, but she had so much money, I couldn't imagine giving her anything material. When she told me about her misplaced bracelet, I wanted to find it for her. We knew it had to be somewhere in her large apartment where there were dozens of places such a bracelet could be lost.

In my heart arose an unshakable determination to find it that summer. It is difficult to describe the quality of my certainty, but I *knew* I would find it no matter what I had to do. As I was drifting off to sleep that same evening, I said aloud, "Jesus, Anthony, Joseph, and whoever else is listening, you've *got* to tell me where that bracelet is!" (Not too humble, right?)

In the twilight just before sleep, an image floated by my awareness. It was a crystal jar with rose petals in the bottom. Suddenly I was bolt awake! That was it! I knew where that jar was. I got up immediately and went fishing among the rose petals. And my fingers found fifty-two sapphires set in platinum. Needless to say, we celebrated late that night!

How often I have wished I could recapture at will the *absolute knowing* I had that day. The incident showed me the direction our trust in God must go if our prayers are going to be effective. The relationship needs to be strong and trusting so we can be certain God cares, hears, and will respond in compassion.

Furthermore, we must be clear both about what we want and the rightness of it. Only then will we be able to believe that God will give it. So when praying for some particular thing or event, we can carefully examine our desire. Only if we know in our very marrow that it is good and right will we be able to pray with the definite conviction that God will give it.

Jesus teaches us also that we must persist in prayer. (See Luke 11:5-8.) He describes tough situations that turn out the way the petitioners wanted because they did not give up. Everyone today seems to want to know why this is so. What is it that persistence does? Well, it has nothing to do with wearing down God's resistance. We know that God never forces us, even into what is absolutely the best for us. God gives more than we ask, sometimes, but the most important developments in discipleship are rarely given unless we ask. This is a *relationship*, not a dictatorship. So when we ask, we enable communication and gift-giving.

Persistence has more to do with what it creates within us. When we persist at something, it becomes more precious to us and we become stronger. Sometimes what we want from God would require a stronger person than we perhaps are yet. Then persistence increases our own readiness. In any case, we can trustfully take Jesus' advice, even if we don't understand just how it works. We can persist in our prayers and expect that God's response will come at the best possible time for us.

The Lord's Prayer

The most familiar of all Jesus' instructions about prayer is, of course, the Lord's Prayer, or the Our Father. Somewhat different memories of it are recorded in Matthew 6:9-13 and in Luke 11:1-4. These differences suggest that Jesus did not intend this prayer primarily as a formula to be repeated verbatim forever. The earliest Christians did not always say it the same way. It is precious to us because it is the only prayer we have from Jesus himself. Still, it was probably meant to be a *pattern* for prayer more than a formal, rote prayer.

What do we learn about prayer in general if we examine the Lord's Prayer as a pattern? If we see the pattern, we can apply it to all of our praying.

Jesus begins by addressing the Father "in heaven," that is, in the spiritual realms. This does not mean that God is in a far-off *place* but rather that God dwells in spirit rather that in a physical situation. It also implies that God, while near enough to be called Father, is beyond us—more than we are, more than we can grasp. Therefore, God is worthy of worship.

That is the next step of the pattern. Jesus offers God honor and recognizes that his name (or essence) is to be kept sacred in the heart, even when God is not understood.

Then Jesus turns our minds to the interests of God. They are our interests too. He prays for the Kingdom to be as full in earthly life as it already is in spiritual realms. That means, among other things, we are invited to pray that the Kingdom will come to fullness within *us*, just as it already is in the realm where God is not resisted as we tend to resist.

This attitude can be ours in any prayer: we want to know God in our hearts, and that happens increasingly as God's Kingdom, or sovereignty, is established in our hearts. In God's own realm of spirit, everything is already totally as God wishes it. We are the ones who tend to skew things, both inside and outside ourselves. When we pray for God's Kingdom within, we pray for the fulfillment of God's will in every aspect of our lives and every atom of our very selves.

So we have prayed for what God wants in us. Now we turn to our own needs: bread for every day. That suggests our physical food and our inner nourishment as well. Everything we need, at every level, is implied here. If we want to list some of them to God, it's a fine thing to do. We can remember, however, that God knows exactly—more exactly than we ourselves know—what we need. So what we do in this petition is open ourselves to God's fulfillment of our daily needs at all levels.

One of our great needs is for our relationship with God to stay straight and open. We break that relationship by sin in act, in attitude, in words. Sin is really whatever interrupts our relationship with God. God will never leave the relationship, but we leave it again and again. Then we must return for forgiveness, for restoration of our relationship. God gives restoration in the measure that we do the same for other people. (Chapter Seven is about forgiveness.)

A couple my husband and I are friends with, who have an idyllic marriage, do this with each other. Every night as they retire, each asks the other if anything was done that day that interrupted their freedom and comfort with each other. Whatever is necessary is described, then forgiven. They sleep in peace, and each day awake closer than they were the day before.

So the pattern here is to keep our side of our relationship with the Lord open by giving forgiveness to others and by asking for it for ourselves. Truly, this would be a wonderful part of any prayer, even if only to keep the channels of communication open.

The last phrases of the prayer ask for help with temptations and trials. Everyone's life has plenty of them. Sometimes God sends them to exercise us into greater strength and willingness for his will. Whether these are daily trials or special events or something at the end of time is not stated. The importance of the pattern is in turning to God about the things we fear and about the events that are troublesome. If we do this habitually, lots of fears and pains find a different place within us or leave entirely. In either case, we are strengthened in God. That's more important than the difficulty itself, isn't it?

Jesus gave his pattern for prayer after the disciples observed Jesus praying and asked him for instruction. The gospels also say that Jesus prayed alone. In Luke 6:12, Jesus is said to have spent all night in prayer. What do you suppose he did all that time? Did he repeat formal prayers? Did he beg over and over for something? What does one do while actually praying all night?

This description suggests that Jesus was a total contemplative. His all-night prayer must have been a prayer of union with God, wordless and without thoughts. He sought total communion of heart and spirit, he went through the night experiencing God, giving himself and receiving God. Who can describe the joys and intimacies of Jesus with his Father?

Many saints across the centuries have experienced this same kind of communion with God, with Christ. Some of them, unlike Jesus, wrote about it so the rest of us can learn to desire and grow into that depth of relationship with God.

Here, as always, Jesus is a model for us. He lived in oneness with God all the time, but still sought solitude so that no distraction or other interest would deter his attention to his loving Father. If Jesus needed it, how much more do we! Yet how far we may seem to be from love intense enough and concentration strong enough to be in conscious closeness with God even for one whole night.

It is a goal to be prayed about. It is a situation to be yearned for. It is a hope offered by Jesus to all his followers who want to live uninterruptedly in the Kingdom.

Ask, and It Will Be Given You

Finally, we come to the last references in these gospels about prayer. Matthew 7:7-11 and Luke 11:9-13 say some of the same things, but there are a couple important differences.

The main point is that prayers are heard. When we ask and seek and knock, we are answered. Even more important, God knows what we need and always gives only good gifts to those who ask and seek. Jesus' Father is not cruel (though life sometimes is) nor neglectful. God sometimes withholds something we think we want because God knows that we would be damaged by it. That is not always apparent to us, but a trusting disciple rightly assumes God's protection.

We are invited to ask in the midst of trusting that God's gifts are always good. When we doubt this about God, it is

41

usually because we haven't gotten something we wanted or because circumstances have brought us pain. We should see that not getting our own way is not a very good reason to doubt God's love and goodness. And besides, our pain is caused more by our own resistance to events than anything else.

Many studies have been done on physical pain and emotional struggles to try to understand pain and how it works. Much remains unknown. One thing is clear, however: when people genuinely relax and accept what is going on, the intensity of pain subsides up to eighty-five percent.

If we trust God and if we practice with small pains, we can learn to let ourselves relax into God a lot sooner than usual. Then we are freed to look for the good gift hidden in every situation that comes along. In the case of death or major injury, this is not expected to be easy. But I'm always reminded of my mother, who suffered with cancer for sixteen years. She said to me once, "If cancer was the only way I could learn what I have learned about God and about myself, I would choose it again."

Of course, we waste much of our pain and difficulties. But when we don't resist them and throw them away, we can always find God's best gifts hidden within them. God *does* give good gifts to his children, and we can know that for ourselves if we are open enough.

Being open is one reason we must ask and seek and knock. Too often we don't really want the things that would be the very best for our own happiness because we don't know in actual fact what is best for our own happiness. But we can open ourselves to the blessings of the Lord by asking for what we do know. Then we are also open to receive whatever he sends.

In Luke, the subject is a little different than our asking for things we want. There Jesus is talking about the supreme gift: the Holy Spirit deep and active in our hearts. It's a gift we, today, believe is given at baptism. Yet how many of us experience the Spirit fully active in our being and our living? Isn't it, for too many of us, a kind of abstraction, something we "believe" in our minds but seldom experience?

If the Holy Spirit is in us but seemingly dormant, we may not experience much help in our everyday search for God's Kingdom inside. It's as if all the ingredients are there, but no one has stirred them together or put them in to bake. So when we ask God for the Holy Spirit and when we apply all that we have just learned about prayer, we can fully expect to have all our ingredients stirred together and baked. That is, the Holy Spirit will begin to guide our lives and to communicate with us in perceivable ways. It will take over as much of the control of our lives as we allow. What a great life we will then have! We will live in the Kingdom, full of God.

All the aspects of prayer that we have seen in the Synoptics overlap and support one another. If we pray in the secret place of our heart and do it persistently, we will learn the secret of Jesus' all-night communion with his Father. If we learn to trust so firmly that all our prayers are empowered by solid expectation, we will be closer to God than we ever imagined. If we put the pattern of the Lord's Prayer into all our praying, it will revolutionize everything, because nothing is left out of that prayer. It sets us in the best situation in relationship to God.

So since we want to be Jesus' disciples and live in the Kingdom, LET US PRAY!

Reflection

1. Think of an incident in your life that taught you about the power of trust in prayer. How can you nurture such trust all the time?

2. What do you think are the hardest aspects of prayer for you? What one step might you take to strengthen yourself?
3. If, as part of every prayer, we pray for God's Kingdom to be full in us, what might happen to our petitions and intentions? Try it for a while and observe the results.
4. Choose one of the prayer-ideas in this chapter that you have little experience with. Begin to practice it. Keep a journal of your experiences as you grow.

CHAPTER FIVE
ACTION FOR THE KINGDOM

The Kingdom is the most desirable life anyone could wish for. It is offered freely by God through Jesus Christ to anyone who sincerely wants it. Still, Kingdom life is never just handed over to anyone. Such a life is too powerful to give to the weak or the unready. To some extent, we are almost all both weak and unready for the full life of the Kingdom. But we are by no means in a hopeless position. We can grow. We can become strong enough. We can get ready.

To be able to receive the Kingdom within ourselves and live from it as our center, we must be active. We must be active in preparation, as we saw in Chapter Three. In Chapter Four, we found that we must be active in prayer. We must ask God for what we want. Now we will look at some beginning principles for further action. According to the Synoptics, there are efforts we must undertake in order to be able to receive God's best gift: life in the Kingdom with Jesus, the Lord of Life.

We Must Act

One of the most puzzling, yet profound, parables Jesus told about life in the Kingdom is found in Luke 16:1-12. Take a moment right now and read it carefully.

At first glance, Jesus seems to commend the steward for a dishonest action. But parables are not analogies to be matched in every imaginable point. This one tells us exactly what the steward is being commended for: his enterprise. The adjective used to describe him has been translated various ways: *prudent, wise, shrewd, astute.*

Jesus is suggesting in the parable that when the steward found himself in a bad corner, he took stock of his real situation (including emotional reactions) and decided to act. He did something calculating and definite—something quite daring, actually—and took a big risk. We may choose to do something honest when we need to help ourselves, but couldn't it be just as clever, just as daring?

Jesus' comment points to the principle that people whose goals are just for this world are often smarter and more active about achieving their goals than people who care about God are in achieving their *much higher* goal. He advises that we learn the principles of this world well and use them, not as goals but as means to the highest goal of all: life in the Kingdom. Above all, be clever and take initiative.

We can observe the condition of the steward in our own lives. We are, in relation to God, far from being what we could be. Are we as shrewd and enterprising in our discipleship as we are in our business or our relationships? Jesus urged his disciples to use the things of this world wisely in light of their goal in the Kingdom. Then when obviously transient interests such as money (you can't take it with you through death!) run out of value, the disciple who has been rightly enterprising will find that the deeper values of life will sustain her or him in God. Through all the lesser concerns, the disciple wants and seeks God. So the disciple attains God.

Another of Jesus' parables shows us that while we may come a long way toward him on the strength of his invitation, unless we are willing to participate fully in the Kingdom we cannot stay. Matthew 22:1-14 is the story of the king who sent out invitations to a wedding. They were refused, so he invited others. But then, at the end, he found one guest inadequately dressed and expelled him.

Precisely what the missing wedding garment signifies is never clear. But it suggests that there are conditions that must be met for the disciple to remain in the celebration of Kingdom life. Those conditions cannot be ignored. Included are a willingness to participate fully and to take action and participate rightly.

Initiative is again praised in Matthew 25:14-30, the familiar parable of the "talents." In Matthew's day, the talent was a unit of money, but today's meaning is just as useful. The Lord has given to everyone particular gifts. Who has the most is of no interest to the Master. What each one actually does with the gifts he or she has is the vital question.

We are both the shrewd steward in the first parable and the gifted employee in this parable. We are in a bad spot, since we often experience ourselves as quite far from God and from God's Kingdom. We also have certain individualized gifts.

We are called to do something: to be clever, to be active, to dare to risk, so we can become greater. In our action, we must be willing to risk losing our smaller self in favor of becoming a bigger self.

Many people simply do not like change; any change at all is experienced as a threat. And it is. Change threatens the smaller self. The third servant did nothing with his gifts because he was afraid. So are we. We are afraid to risk losing what we have for the mere possibility that we might be able to make it into much more. This attitude is not acceptable to the Lord.

The Lord asks us to move! Let go of the past, let go of our smallness, and act on our own behalf in relationship to God. No one else can do what needs to be done to bring us into the Kingdom. We must act for ourselves. That is one of the most important aspects of our call to God's Kingdom. Our yes cannot be only in words. It must be in daring and clever actions as well.

We Must Receive

Jesus went about the country doing good things for people. He healed their blindness, their lameness, their deafness, their diseases. He freed them from emotional and mental disturbances, from violent inner struggles. He cured their moral deficiencies and made of them generous people. He fed people in great crowds—performed amazing acts just to give people lunch.

In short, Jesus gave to people. Jesus took care of people. Does he do the same for you? Before you answer too quickly, think: do you allow the Lord to heal all your ills and weaknesses? Do you allow the Lord to be your number one nourisher?

If you question whether the Lord helps you in these ways, your experiences are probably mixed. You have prayed for help, perhaps, and were not healed or fed. Or maybe you know people to whom that has happened. Much is uncertain in our understanding of healing.

One thing is sure, however: the Lord is more ready to give than we are ready to receive. Readiness means more than wishing. It means being *able* to assimilate the gift and to keep it with gratitude, certitude, and respect. Those qualities have to be within us, ready for use as it were, before certain experiences can be given. The more we can do to strengthen ourselves, the more ready we will be to receive.

Do we already live with deeply grateful hearts? Do we already receive blessings with deep certainty that they come from the Lord? Do we already receive all gifts with respect for the divine Giver? These questions can suggest practices you can take up to strengthen yourself enough to be able to receive *all* of the Lord's graciously given healing and nourishment within your being. Receiving is discipleship too.

We Tend to Our Own Path

"If your eye is healthy, your whole body is full of light; but if it is not healthy, your body is full of darkness. Therefore consider whether the light in you is not darkness" (Luke 11:34-35). Jesus is saying here that to live in the inner Kingdom, we have to take care of our own state of being.

We already have light within us. It may be deeply hidden even from ourselves, but everyone has light within. If our lives, our face, our eyes, are not full of shining light, then it is merely veiled from our awareness. But those veils can be tough and opaque! The light of God lives in us, probably by creation itself, certainly by baptism. It will never go out, this holy flame.

But what good does it do us if our inner eyes are closed or damaged? We need the healing of Jesus more in our awareness of inner divine light than in any other part of our being. That light is essential. It shows us the way to the Kingdom. It expands, so to speak, and becomes the Kingdom in our own hearts.

Here's another way to think of it. It is like a path of light overgrown by briars and burrs and thick thornbushes. Until we tend that path and open it to our own feet, we will neither see its light nor be able to follow the way.

Every effort we make toward fuller discipleship will help clear our path and reveal the light in our own being. One specific way to tend your path, your state of being, is to pull out and toss aside all negative, complaining reactions to people, to the news, to circumstances. To some, it may sound shallow to replace every negative thought with a positive one. They are mistaken. It is not a complex theory, but practicing it successfully is neither easy nor obvious. For those who do it, light fills their lives—that very light that has lived hidden in the depths of their being. Then they can put their light on the stand, for all to see and enjoy.

Be Generous of Heart

That simple act of allowing one's true light to shine on all via positive thoughts and feelings is one lovely way of being generous of heart. Another is to watch one's speech about others. Speech, of course, comes from attitudes. The first disciples had to learn this too.

Read Luke 9:52-55. It shows Jesus' attitude toward the slightest thought of ugliness or vindictiveness toward others. What other attitudes, what other kinds of speech do you imagine Jesus would decidedly rebuke?

Recently, my husband objected to something I had done. He was not unkind, but I flared into raised-voice self-defense. Afterward, I felt as ashamed as if Jesus had rebuked me right there. Perhaps he did, in my heart. It burned.

I had not caught the negative before it pushed into the situation. Since it still burns when I recall it, perhaps the fire will burn the negative impulse to a cinder and self-defensiveness will be gradually removed. Or perhaps I will catch myself before I speak and give myself time to reenvision the inner light and let that shine instead.

Generosity of heart, followed to its ultimate quality in the

Kingdom, means loving all without regard to their attitudes toward us. Luke 6:27 begins a paragraph that describes various aspects of this generous love. The same subject is discussed in Matthew 5:43-45. How is such love possible?

It will not be possible for us as long as we assume that loving has something to do with whether the loved one deserves it or not. God's love for us does not depend on what kind of person we are *at all*. Thank goodness! God loves because it is his nature to love. Neither credit nor blame is ours. God loves us.

In years past, I sometimes visited people in state prisons. I used to wonder about the mothers who faithfully came each week to visit their convicted sons. A few of them told me their stories. If someone had asked whether the men deserved their mothers' love, the answer would often have been a flat no. The mothers loved their sons because *their* own hearts were loving. That's all that is necessary.

When we allow our own hearts to become loving hearts, we cannot hold love in or parcel it out according to some personal judgment or even according to what a person has done to us. We choose to love, or we don't choose to love. It is a direct choice. Before we choose too quickly, it might be a good idea to consider this: a heart closed to some cannot be fully open to God's love.

A heart full of love simply gives. It does not worry about the results of that giving or about whether it will receive something in return. In fact, Jesus explicitly says that it is better to give love to those who will certainly not return it. As my friend, psychotherapist Mary Shea, says, "If you give out of one pipe and expect it to come back through another, you have no more than you began with. But if you give without expectations, your pipe gets gold-plated as your love goes through it."

Gold-plated pipes? For me, that's another way of describing a heart that is so generous to others that it can live inwardly full of God. For God is love and God's Kingdom is divine love permeating a whole life.

Letting Go of Results

Jesus poses an interesting question in Matthew 24:45-46. "Who then is the faithful and wise slave, whom his master has put in charge of his household, to give the other slaves their allowance of food at the proper time? Blessed is that slave whom his master will find at work when he arrives."

Each of us who wants to live in the Kingdom is that slave, in charge of whatever part of the whole house the Lord has given us. We may have a huge dining room full of dozens of people to feed, or we may have been given a small corner with one or two. The size of our charge does not matter. Will we distribute food to them—physical food, emotional food, spiritual food—as it is needed? Will we do so simply because the master has left them in our charge?

Notice that Jesus does not say we are responsible for how well our nourishment is received, nor are we to expect gratitude in return. We are responsible to feed. The results of that feeding are up to God, just as much as the results of planting a seed in spring are up to God. It is our charge from the Lord to develop a generous heart and give without concern for results.

Leaving the results up to the Lord is just another way of saying, "Thy will be done." Taking care of our particular charge is a way of doing God's will.

Mark 3:31-35 is familiar to all of us because it is one of the few passages that mentions Jesus' mother. We have so often heard that blood kinship did not mean as much to Jesus as the kinship of those who do the will of God. Mary must have understood this too. Certainly it is a great hope for us, isn't it? If we do the will of God, and allow *all* of God's will to be done in and through us, we will be claimed as sister and brother by the Lord. We will always be welcome in his own household.

Jesus himself gave his whole being constantly to the will of the Father. He actively did it by following every inner hint the Father gave him. He actively took care of people in need. He taught. In the end, he gave the largest, most potent gift possible: his life. He did it only because it became obvious that this, too, was the will of God. (See Matthew 26:39.) To live in Jesus' Kingdom will mean, finally, a willingness to do the will of God no matter what it is. Then not only the willingness, but the actual doing—as actual as physical death if that is required.

That is a phenomenal challenge, isn't it? It is the fulfillment of leaving the results up to God. If we give ourselves to God, it means that even the way of our death is God's to choose. Can we be content with that?

Every Step Overlaps Every Other Step

The wonderful quality about moving toward life in the Kingdom, toward full discipleship, is that we can begin anywhere. The way is so rich, as it is explained, hinted at, and promoted in the Synoptics, that we can begin wherever we wish. It is a little like stepping on to a slowly circling platform. No matter where we enter the circle, it will take us all the way around if we stay with it. We must take that first step though.

If in reading this book up to this point, you have found an idea or a practice that opened your heart or suggested a new perspective, take that as your next step, even before you read any further. Make it real. Actualize it by doing some concrete thing of your own clever invention.

Then when you have learned what that arc of the circle has to teach you at this time, you can move to the next most attractive idea and begin to put some inventive effort into that step. Continuing this way, the circle of grace will move you, and you will be cooperating by moving with it.

Reflection

1. Will the Master find you distributing food when he suddenly comes? What part of the Lord's house is yours to care for? Perhaps it is a part that no one else cares for, or perhaps there are others. Name the people and situations in your charge.
2. If you gave the same amount of thought, attention, and creativity to your career as you do to your life as a disciple, what would happen to your career?
3. If you do not experience God's love in great flowing fullness all the time, to whom or to what have you closed your own heart? What do you wish to do about that?
4. Recall your conversations with your family during the last week. What would Jesus have said about your speech and its underlying attitudes?

CHAPTER SIX

MORE PRINCIPLES OF LIFE IN THE KINGDOM

If disciples are people who love others and who consciously seek the Kingdom of God within, they are also people who are wide awake and paying attention according to the Synoptics. We have seen already that initiative and action are important to becoming effective disciples. The gospels give more principles for the growth of life in the Kingdom.

Waking Up

One kind of required action is simply to *wake up*! Many of us would protest "But I am awake! And if I'm not awake, then what does waking up mean?"

This principle is multileveled. We can be a teeny bit awake or fully awake or somewhere in between. There is more than one kind of wakefulness, and there is more than one kind of sleep. "Waking up," as used here, does not refer to getting out of bed each day with our physical eyes more or less open.

We might compare it to an incident involving two friends watching the performance of a musical play. While the leading lady is singing, she has to throw a cup at her partner. But at this performance, she misses and the cup falls over the edge of the stage and hits the clarinetist on the head. Everybody gasps. Afterward, one friend laughs over the incident. The other doesn't remember it, though, because she was not paying attention to the action at that point. She was studying the pattern on the dress of the woman in front of her. Her eyes were open, but she was asleep to the events on stage. Her attention was elsewhere.

Jesus told several stories urging his disciples to stay awake! Pay attention! Be alert! These stories are sometimes in the context of the expected end of time and final coming of the Lord. When we consider them in the context of the Kingdom, however, we easily see that the Lord comes to each of us in unexpected ways and at unexpected times. One of my own strongest experiences of the Lord's presence occurred when I was brushing my teeth after supper one evening. Had I been engrossed in thinking about something in particular at that moment, I might have missed the Lord's coming to me. We have all probably missed him hundreds of times—not because he does not come to us, but because our attention is elsewhere and we do not perceive his presence.

The Synoptics give us hints about the forms of sleep we might look for in our lives. When we see how we are asleep, we can begin to invent ways to help ourselves wake up.

One form of sleepiness that affects us is a kind of carelessness or an assumption that we don't need to prepare for the unexpected. Matthew 25:1-13 tells the familiar story of the ten virgins waiting for the bridegroom. Half of them brought extra oil for their lamps so when the hour got late they were ready, they still had light. The others had to go off and seek more oil. While they were gone, the groom came and the door was barred behind the prepared women. The unprepared ones got locked out of the celebration.

We too easily expect that the Lord might come to us during a special time, such as when we're praying. Or we imagine the Lord will come in a particular way. Whatever we imagine, the Lord's coming will almost certainly be different. If we are to be aware of the Lord's presence when he offers himself to us, we need to practice preparing for a long wait. We need to drop our expectations about the time or the form of the Lord's action inside us. We must invent ways to prepare for any eventuality and to keep ourselves ready to rejoice with him when he arrives.

Another form of sleepiness is implied in Mark 13:33-37. Here Jesus uses the figure of the servants being left, each with a responsibility, while the master goes on a trip. Since the servants don't know when the master is returning, the wise ones don't go to sleep on their job. They remain diligent and fulfill their responsibilities without procrastination. Laziness and procrastination are forms of sleep, based on the assumption that one can hurry up and get it done just before the master returns.

Being awake has to do with being able to receive the Lord when he gives himself to us. Certain skills are involved in that receiving, as we have already seen. We must be ready, or the beautiful experience of welcoming him cannot occur. If we procrastinate in our responsibilities or if we are lazy, he will come and know that we have not done our part, because we will not be ready to welcome him into our heart. This kind of sleep keeps us wandering unconcernedly through our life, unready to receive the Lord, figuring it will all happen much later anyhow (like after death!). That's often why we miss out on the splendid possibilities of life with Christ right now.

Luke 12:35 adds another idea. Here Jesus commends the

one who is still awake and on the job, even in the middle of the night or at any other inconvenient time. Imagine that a voice asked you right now, "Shall the Lord come to you this very hour?" How many of us would answer, "Please don't come until next week. Today is not a good time for me to have guests."

Jesus remarks on how blessed are those who stay awake even in the midst of inconvenience—or even in their own time for bodily sleep—ready to welcome him instantly, to drop every other interest and just be hospitable to the Lord.

Along with the question of general inconvenience is a reference to our tendency to get so caught up in the cares of a super-busy life that we make no room to be alert to the Lord. We simply forget about God because we are so involved in everything else. (See Luke 21:34.) It is as if we are drunk on everyday living and miss the deepest dimension of it: attention to the Lord, being awake to the Lord's presence.

One of the many ways we can help ourselves stay awake is to check the fruit we have borne each day. Jesus reminds us that only good trees bear good fruit. (See Matthew 12:33-37.) If we want to know how "good" we are, how awake we are, how free we are from drowsiness and being lost in daily affairs, we can check ourselves. Every evening we can take a few minutes to review the day. Let's not make a hunt for sin; let's simply look to see when we were awake and ready for the Lord in any form of communication and when we were utterly forgetful and asleep to him.

We don't need to do anything more than notice what our day has been like. If we do not find the good fruit we'd like to find, we may offer the whole situation gently to the Lord and let it go.

If we do this every evening for a while, the changes in attentiveness during the day will soon come of themselves. We do not need to force them. Awareness is a powerful agent for changing. Awareness is more powerful in the long run than any attempt at forcing ourselves to try to be different, especially with subtle inner acts like waking up.

Staying With It

Some of the principles of the Kingdom are not unlike the principles for any kind of success—except that we *expect* them to be different. Somehow we are often willing to work many hours a week for years and years to be strong in our career or our relationships, but we assume that spiritual strength and attainment will (or should) come quickly and easily. That is simply an error.

The love of God for us is a given. We do not have to earn it. We cannot earn it. But being big enough ourselves to receive all the Lord has to give is a lifelong adventure in growing. A spiritual teacher once asked her students what they wanted when they became her students. One of them said that he didn't think he should want anything, but should just be ready to receive all the teacher could give him. The teacher quietly asked, "How big is your bag?"

How much are we able to receive of God? To create a big bag, Jesus says, we must persist. We must keep doing everything that can lead to growth—and keep doing it and keep doing it. After Jesus tells the familiar parable of the sower in Luke 8:4-8, he tells his followers what he meant by the seed that fell on rich soil. They "are the ones who, when they hear the word, hold it fast in an honest and good heart, and bear fruit with patient endurance" (8:15).

In a way, it's very simple. A runner gets to the finish line by putting one foot in front of the other over and over and over again.

Today, the notion of persistence over time to meet a goal is not supported by our ordinary cultural experience. In entertainment, in the media presentations of almost any subject, in all advertising and much technology, the emphasis is on speed: do it now, get it now, this instant. Don't wait. And (worse) if you can't get it now, it's not what you want. And (even worse yet) if you don't get it now, you'll fail at life!

Yet we know from experience that those things or situations we work for and wait for and sacrifice for are the truly important factors in our lives. Nothing of lasting value is attained quickly. Persistence gives us strength. It teaches us patience. It makes mature human beings of us.

In the spirituality of the Synoptics, persistence brings success in the one area that matters for all eternity: closeness to the Lord himself.

Be Like a Child

If persistence is easily understood (though not always gladly performed), Jesus' next idea is a little trickier. Read Matthew 18:1-4. Here the disciples are interested in the nature of greatness in the Kingdom. Unfortunately, they were especially interested in *who* among them would be the greatest. (See // Mark 9:33-37 and // Luke 9:46-48.)

In this context, though the individual stories vary a little, Jesus places a child among the disciples. Just what is it about a child that Jesus approves? The answer to that question has differed with the interests of various interpreters.

For our purposes, one principle Jesus is pointing to is a certain humility. Children in Jesus' time had no social standing, no "rights." If their parents treated them well, they were fortunate, but advocates of a happy childhood did not exist. Children played their way into adulthood and were expected to achieve social learning along the way. Children were almost not regarded as real people.

That sociological fact contains a clue to Jesus' meaning. Since he uses a child—a social nobody—as a perfect example of greatness in the Kingdom, we may understand him to be directly repudiating the very notion of social greatness in any circumstance. In Luke 14:10, Jesus advises voluntarily taking the lowest places.

What is at the root of a desire for social status? Isn't it pride or the wish for recognition? Jesus, however, recommends the very opposite: no pride, no desire for status. Just live your life, be humble, volunteer for the service jobs, and take no credit. Just *be*, in the way that a child often just *is*. The child lives life from inner motives, whatever they may be, and appears to be absorbed simply in the moment. That's the picture of freedom from ego-investment that Jesus places before his disciples.

A wonderful example of this kind of service is Saint Therese, the Little Flower. She wanted to be a missionary but was in a cloister. Her service of personal sanctification and prayer for the missions was deeply hidden behind walls. Her approach to her own position was the "little way," grounded in compassion. She assumed that she herself needed to be humbler and more hidden. If you want a picture of a person who has taken this single approach to sanctity and arrived there, she is one of the best. Her autobiography is wonderful inspiration and instruction.

When one's energies are directed toward discipleship for the sake of the Kingdom, the ego is gradually displaced from its central and dominating position. That means not only that we seek the lowest places but that we live so much in the moment with the Lord's presence that we are not interested at all in position, low or high. We are freed from that kind of arrogance to live simply a moment at a time. It is as beautiful as the most beautiful childhood, probably even more lovely that any real childhood ever was.

Be Grateful

Once Jesus healed ten lepers. Only one came back to thank him, which he found surprising. (See Luke 17:11-19.) The message is simple: give thanks for everything, all the time, everywhere. Entire books have been written about the attitude of thankfulness. Simply and directly, the basic message here is this: do it.

Gratitude opens the heart. An open heart is necessary to receive the Kingdom. Gratitude is an act of love. God is love. Gratitude acknowledges our interdependence with all that exists. We are part of a network of life that extends to every plant or animal—everything that is part of this universe in which we live. Nothing is truly separate from anything else.

The Hindus have a wonderful image for this. It symbolizes the universe as a net, like a giant fishnet. At every juncture of the cords is a diamond cut round, totally clear, and reflective of everything. If one puts a dot on one of these diamonds, every other diamond shows a dot too. If one pushes on one cord, the whole net vibrates.

That's life. Nothing is isolated, certainly not a human being! It behooves us to be grateful for the whole and to express our gratitude to the divine Creator of it all. Without any of it, we could not be. Without this awareness of the whole, we cannot fully live in the Kingdom. The Kingdom of love demands alertness to loving all that exists. If we shut out any part, no matter how small, we close down just that much of our own heart—and so close the door to our own awareness of the Kingdom. Gratitude for all, all the time, keeps all doors open and keeps awareness of our shared existence keenly alive.

Take Rest in the Lord

Have you ever, at the end of a harried day, sank into a sofa and wished with all your heart for a long, uninterrupted rest—longer than a night and maybe even longer than a vacation? The Kingdom of the Lord is a kingdom of rest. Perhaps that is one reason so many people tend to push the Kingdom into the hereafter. They cannot imagine such rest ever being possible in this world.

Jesus said otherwise: "Come to me, all you that are weary and are carrying heavy burdens, and I will give you rest. Take my yoke upon you, and learn from me; for I am gentle and humble in heart, and you will find rest for your souls" (Matthew 11:28-29).

He did not mean at some distant future date. He meant now, if we want it. For rest or living without burdens is almost entirely a matter of attitude. Our burdens do not really come, for example, from having too much to do. They come from *feeling* that we are overladen. Our burdens do not even come from pain, but from resisting our pain.

The story is told of a farmer whose life looked extremely hard. His soil was poor. He managed to support himself and his wife, but barely. His wife was an invalid and required extra care. They lived some distance from any village, so routine supplies were not easy to bring home. Theirs was a life of toil and effort and poverty.

One day, the elders of the village came to ask the farmer a question that had been bothering them. They had heard a priest say that suffering did not need to make one feel unhappy or oppressed. They did not understand that statement, but they thought this farmer might, because he always seemed so cheerful. But when they asked him their question, he said he couldn't answer it.

They pushed him. "I'm so sorry, my friends," he said again.

"You have come to the wrong person. I cannot answer your question, because you see, I am not suffering!"

Some people carry what seem to be heavy loads, but they carry them with a light and trusting heart, so they are not burdened by them. Others carry less troublesome loads that seem huge because their hearts are doubt-filled and they resist their daily tasks.

Jesus promised that if people learned from him—which means putting his principles into practice—they would no longer be burdened, but restful of heart. He did not say what their circumstances would be like, but he promised that the dreadful compulsions and striving and worried attitudes would not be in those hearts.

When the heart is at peace because it lives in love and in joy—because it lives in God—then the body continues with life according to its natural rhythms and *all is well*. Everything is easier, and whatever loads we are asked to carry seem light to us instead of oppressive. Yes, it can be done. It *is* done all the time by those who have yoked themselves to the Lord, who have joined their lives to God.

This possibility is graphically illustrated by the familiar scene of Jesus in the home of Mary and Martha of Bethany. (See Luke 10:38:42.) Jesus is commonly misunderstood to mean that service is inferior to contemplation. That is an incorrect interpretation, however. Jesus does not object to Martha's serving but to her anxiety and her habit of worrying. He says that there is actual need of only one thing and that is loving attention to the Lord.

When one's top priority is the Lord, the heart can live in trustful rest, even if the person is busy in serving others, taking care of a household, and earning a living. The intent here is not to divide the so-called "active" life from the so-called "contemplative" life. Rather, the contemplative attitude of listening and trust is the only requirement, and whatever action is needed will follow from that Kingdom-oriented choice.

Reflection

1. For two days, notice when you go "on automatic pilot" in your work, your driving, or your play. Notice how often you are aware of what is happening in this very moment and how often you only recall it later. What is the quality of those moments of automatism (or sleep) compared to those of lucidity (being awake)?
2. Take an honest look at the intensity of gratitude in your daily life. Is it a constant attitude? an occasional "Thanks, God?" a weekly warm feeling for a remembered event? How grateful are you?
3. When is your heart at rest? How often? Notice why it is at rest and why it is not at rest. Allow yourself to experience the difference. Check your body for tension, your mind for worries or striving, your emotions for hyperactivity. Is there a great calm underlying everything you do? You may want to put your findings into prayer.

CHAPTER SEVEN

FORGIVENESS, THE BOTTOM LINE

Matthew tells us that Jesus understood his death to be "for the forgiveness of sins" (Matthew 26:28). If Jesus came to die so that sins would be forgiven, he must also have lived for forgiveness. He must have come to demonstrate forgiveness by forgiving, as well as to teach his disciples to forgive.

Because forgiveness is central to Jesus' death and life, it is necessarily central to the spiritual life of the disciple. Forgiveness begins with Jesus and God. Moreover, forgiveness is always available, because the Lord is essentially forgiving. However, as we have seen, we never receive the great spiritual gifts easily or automatically. We must be ready and able to receive them. Matthew and Luke both record that Jesus stated strongly that the disciple will (or can be) forgiven by God only when that disciple has forgiven all others. (Read Matthew 6:14-15 and Luke 11:4; also Mark 11:25.)

Since we regularly pray the Our Father, which reminds us that we are forgiven as we forgive others, we must be open to

learning everything we can about forgiveness and then doing it.

An Act of Grace

Forgiveness is essentially an act of grace. That is, the forgiven one has done something that does not deserve loving
kindness, but the other lives so deeply in love that the love in
the relationship is more important than what the wrong-doer
deserves.

I once heard a speaker tell of an experience from his childhood. About age nine, he got angry one day with his mother
because she wouldn't let him do what he wanted to do. So he
quietly went into her bedroom, found a pair of scissors, and
cut off all of her dresses just below the waist.

When his mother discovered what he had done, he had
carefully hidden himself in another closet. But she burst into
tears, and he was unable to stay away. When she saw him,
she gathered him into her arms, still weeping, and said, "Billy,
what did I do to you that made you so angry?" That, said the
speaker, is the grace of forgiveness.

The first understanding that we need to hold with total
clarity is that God is pure compassion, so God is always ready
to forgive us. Indeed, what reader of this book can say that
forgiveness has not been offered countless times for our foolish wrongs? The question is, have we received it?

If we have not practiced forgiving others, we are not able
genuinely and effectively to receive God's beautiful, loving
forgiveness of us when we are wrong.

We may ask about forgiveness like Peter did. He wanted
to know from Jesus how many times a disciple is required to
forgive. Jesus replied that we are to forgive without limit—
over and over again—for as long as wrongs are done. Then
he went on to tell Peter and the others the parable about the

unforgiving servant, which makes it absolutely clear that God's forgiveness and human forgiveness are bound to each other. (See Matthew 18:21-35.) Disciples who long for life in the Kingdom forgive everyone, all the time.

One statement in this parable can be puzzling. In verse 34, the master in the story turns the unforgiving one "over to be tortured." It is a harsh image. Jesus did not mean that God is vengeful. He was acutely aware, however, that people who do not forgive do, in fact, live in torture—inner torture.

Today it is well-known that many diseases are anger-related. Anger that is kept, held, and nurtured makes the physical body sick. That is one kind of "torture."

Kept anger also means that there are little sections of our hearts that we must keep walled off because they are so painful. The more angers and grudges we cling to, the less of our heart can be open to receive God's love and to give love. The source of our greatest joys is gradually choked off by unforgiveness.

An acquaintance of mine destroyed a friendship of many years by holding a grudge over something he thought had been done to him. He did not bother to check with the other person; he just held on to his anger. And the broken relationship tortured him in a hundred ways. He is still tortured about it after more than twenty-five years. All that pain could have been avoided, all could have been resolved, by an act of obedience to the Lord, an act of forgiveness. It's one of the saddest things I know when someone wrecks his or her own peace by refusing to forgive.

Will it cost us something inwardly to forgive another person? Yes and no. It will feel costly at first because our egocentricity will flare up and begin to burn. The burning will not be pleasant. But if we are willing to stay with it, to persist in our forgiveness, peace will come.

And more than peace. Our ego-centeredness will have lost

some of its power: a situation we are all aiming for anyway if we are devoted to living in the Kingdom. We want the ego to be displaced from domination; we want power over our selfishness. Forgiving will give us that power in large chunks at a time.

We need to realize this: when we forgive someone, we are not doing it so much for that person's benefit as for our own. Eventually, we may grow to the point where forgiveness just naturally flows and blame does not even arise in the heart any more. But until then, we practice forgiving because if we don't, our relationship with God is interrupted. Our determination to live in the Kingdom is broken by an unforgiving attitude. Then God, once again, seems very far away. But we have only shut God out; God hasn't gone away. God waits. God waits for us to "get it," to forgive so that our relationship can be restored.

Choosing to Forgive

We sometimes find it difficult to forgive because we equate the act of forgiveness with mustering up positive emotions about the hurt. It very rarely works that way. Forgiveness is a spiritual fact long before it becomes an emotional experience. Forgiveness is rooted in the will, in our capacity to choose our attitudes. We all have that capacity. It is up to us whether we exercise it or not.

When we choose to forgive, that is, when we are fully willing to let go of our anger and our hurt feelings over whatever has been done to us, we are *actually* forgiving. Our choice is made. Then we can pray to the Lord and say, "I choose to forgive so-and-so. I do not wish to hold on to anger or emotional hurt. Please take care of what needs to be done." Such a prayer is always heard. Forgiveness in that moment is a fact.

What happens when we see the person who has wronged

us the next day, maybe unexpectedly? Chances are, our emotions will jump into the situation again. What we do then is crucial. If we begin to berate ourselves for not *feeling* forgiveness emotionally, we effectively retract our prayer of forgiveness. We can, if we wish, acknowledge immediately to the Lord that the anger has arisen again and ask again that it be removed. We can reaffirm our forgiveness. Then it may be helpful to go do something else that requires our attention so we don't bog down in our emotions all over again.

Little by little, the emotions will subside and disappear if they are not fed. We can repeat this basic process as often as needed until we experience true and complete peacefulness. Meanwhile, we will be able to pray the Our Father freely and honestly once again!

When we are freed inside, we can accept God's forgiveness. Accepting God's forgiveness of us is another way of saying that we are willing to forgive ourselves, that we are willing to live in a forgiving stance that includes ourselves. After all, it is only a peculiar kind of pride that refuses to forgive oneself.

It is deeply humbling to forgive oneself, especially if one has a keen sense of wrong done to another person. Self-forgiveness is not simply taking our own foolishness for granted. It is a recognition that we want to be better than we are. We feel remorse when we do wrong. It is an admission that we are weak and we *need* the Lord's forgiveness. Self-forgiveness is not excusing ourselves but accepting ourselves with the weaknesses we have and the shortcomings of which we are aware.

Forgiveness is like a circle. God's forgiveness of us, our forgiveness of others, and acceptance of God's forgiveness and forgiving ourselves because it is God's will—all these are closely tied to one another. If one is missing, all are weakened in our experience.

Forgiving, then, is a central principle of living close to the Lord. The Synoptic Gospels make such strong statements about it that we have to say that forgiveness is not optional. It is a kind of bottom line. Either we are willing to practice and learn it, or we are not. If we are not, we are shutting the door to the Kingdom right in our own faces.

A Great Flow of Love

Jesus forgave his torturers from the cross. (See Luke 23:34.) He was able to do so in this extreme moment because he had always done so; it was part of his character. By then, he would not even have considered *not* forgiving them. If Jesus arrived at this beautiful point, then we are invited to follow him—to practice forgiving until it becomes a constant, unbroken attitude that blesses everyone around us all the time.

The practice of forgiveness, over and over again, eventually becomes a great flow of love in our lives. The wise and saintly say that one day we can become so thoroughly forgiving that we will be able to love all people equally without reference to our personal judgments of their character and without thinking about the way they treat us. We develop a total attitude of forgiveness that no one can damage.

What is this attitude but pure love? Jesus was once asked about the greatest commandment of all. His answer is one you know well: love the Lord above all, and love your neighbor as you love yourself. (See Matthew 22:36-39.)

Psychologists today tell us that in fact we do love others the way we love ourselves because we cannot love others any better than we are able to love ourselves. Jesus, of course, meant that we should care as actively for others as we take care of our own interests. Yet the psychological point is a good one too. It certainly applies to the flow of love released by forgiveness.

If we forgive others all the time, we are open to loving them without hindrance. If we forgive ourselves, we will forgive others more easily. Then we and they together can bask in the constant love and forgiveness of the Lord without erecting walls against it. Our love and the Lord's love will then flow as one beautiful stream from our hearts into every corner of our world.

The profound connection between forgiving and receiving forgiveness, and loving and receiving love, is reflected in the story about Jesus in Luke 7:36-48. This version of Jesus' feet being washed by a "sinful woman," probably a known prostitute, ties love and forgiveness together as one. She is forgiven because she loves much; she doesn't even have to ask for forgiveness. On the other hand, if one is forgiven little, one also loves very little. It's like a positive Catch-22, isn't it? At whichever point one begins, the other follows without hindrance.

Working for Justice From a Loving Heart

Growing in love for God and neighbor sometimes leaves us feeling we are not doing enough for the world. Think about it for a moment. If we are practicing forgiveness, working toward developing an attitude of total and constant loving forgiveness, then we are helping the world. We are taking anger and other ugliness out of our corner of the world. We are releasing other people from bondage to their mistakes, as well as ourselves. Our relationships will all be more loving. We will not be spewing misplaced or repressed anger. What a blessing that is for people we meet and people we live with!

Further, as the practice of forgiveness becomes more constant, it spreads in other ways. We begin to live with a kindly heart in regard to people whose wrongdoing was not directed at us and did not affect us particularly. We can forgive leaders of Church and state when they are foolish, we can forgive the crimes committed everywhere every day, we can forgive the negligence and wrongs that fill our newscasts and magazines.

Does forgiving mean not working to improve conditions? Does it mean not challenging the leaders to become better? No. Forgiveness is not a slide into complacency. But forgiving means we begin to work for justice from a loving heart, a heart that loves *all*, not just those on our side and not just those who have been wronged.

Mahatma Gandhi was not a Christian, but he understood this principle. More than once, when a political figure whose habits he was opposing became ill or had other serious problems, Gandhi called off his action until health and quiet returned. He loved his opponents. That's why he did them no violence. That's also why he was able to accomplish as much as he did. In addition to his more well-known political victories in India, Gandhi laid the foundations of today's progress against apartheid in South Africa.

When those who work for justice adopt anger and violence as principles or tactics, they violate the spirit of forgiveness, which for Christians is not an option. If Christians say they want the Kingdom but continue to keep and foster their angers, and refuse to forgive, they are deluding themselves. Yes, it is a strong statement, but one totally supported by the Jesus of the Synoptic Gospels.

Reflection

1. Recall a time when you forgave freely just because you loved someone—a child, a spouse, a friend. What was the quality of your experience?
2. If you have not practiced forgiveness very much, ponder how much you have been forgiven by God. See if you can

find connections in your experience. If you believe yourself to have been forgiven often, have you passed that forgiveness on unstintingly? Your reflections may lead you to prayer.

3. Often it is the sheer injustice in a situation that gives us an excuse not to forgive. If you are living with this kind of unforgiveness, take time to ponder deeply Jesus' forgiveness from the cross. Where was justice? What was Jesus' attitude?

CHAPTER EIGHT

OBSTACLES CAN BE HEALED

If the path to the Kingdom is within us, and if the goal in Kingdom life is equally within us, then the obstacles to the Kingdom will also be found within us.

When we assume that the quality of our life is determined by outside circumstances, we are likely to feel trapped, as if we had no power to improve our lives. This is a false perception. When we truly discover, usually after a long time, that our life experiences are determined from within, we simultaneously discover the source of our own power for goodness.

Thus, when obstacles to life in the Kingdom arise, no matter where they initially seem to come from, we can uncover their root within ourselves. Then we can set about cutting out that root or offering it to the Lord for healing. Like all the Lord's gifts, healing is sure to come, *and* we must cooperate with God's giving.

Fear and Doubt

Two of the most deeply rooted obstacles to Kingdom life are fear and doubt. Everyone experiences these two inner obstacles. Sometimes we capitulate to them. Sometimes we live beyond them. Some people discover that the forces latent in fear and doubt can be harnessed for love and trust. Those are the people who learn the ways of the Kingdom. Other people find that they can turn over their fears and doubts to the Lord, who will heal them and give them new experiences. They, too, come to the Kingdom—perhaps even more quickly than those who try to do it themselves.

Let's look a little at the nature of these two obstacles—get acquainted with the enemy a bit so to speak.

Masters of the spiritual life say that fear will be with us to some degree until we have experienced the death of the ego-centric aspect of ourselves. As long as we are interested in our own welfare, fear will remain. Personally, I know that fearlessness is a great virtue that I must attend to, because fear has not departed from my life. It is, however, much lessened compared even to five years ago. The change is beauty; it is hope for more.

We experience fear in the whole being. It is a profound emotion, necessary at a certain level for survival (or so we assume—erroneously). When we are afraid, our thoughts, our memories, our bodies, our emotions—everything—gets into upheaval. This almost instinctive reaction to *perceived* threat is a total readiness to act and act quickly. Whether one chooses to fight the threat or to flee it, action is required.

Why is fear an obstacle to the Kingdom? For one thing, it is biologically impossible for fear and love to exist at the same moment in the same person. The chemical reactions to these states are mutually exclusive. If love is the quality of the Kingdom, then fear keeps us out.

Fear is also centered on the self rather than on the Lord. Fear, at its root, has to do with *my* things, *my* beliefs, *my* survival, *my* desires, *my* imagination. When the focus is different, even for a short time, fear will diminish or leave altogether.

Doubt is equally centered on the little self. It worries about "what is going to happen to me" or that "maybe I'm not good enough." There are lots of other doubts and worries. Because the little self does not understand or cannot control something, it imagines all kinds of negative outcomes. Deep self-doubt leads to no action in life. Doubt of God is basically a reflection of self-doubt. Doubt also hampers love.

Fear and doubt both hamper faith. In fact, we might say they are both opposites to faith, just as they are opposites to love. They especially oppose the aspect of faith that is trustfulness.

When the disciples found themselves puzzled by Jesus' power or when they tried to do something powerful and failed, Jesus called them "you of little faith." When they were immobilized by fear, Jesus said the same thing to them.

Fear and doubt are enemies of the Kingdom because they shut down our hearts into tight knots. Then the love and power of God cannot flow, neither for our own sakes nor for anyone else.

Fear and doubt can be healed, however. Whether or not they ever totally disappear from our life, we can come a long, long way toward a different life-stance—a Kingdom life-stance. We can live in faith, in trust, and in love as constant experiences.

Focus on the Lord

One thing we can do to help ourselves is simply change our focus. When our thoughts are focused on fear and doubt, we give them free opportunity to reign in our living. When our thoughts are habitually focused on the Lord, faith, trust, and love grow naturally within us.

Once my husband, John, was walking downtown amid big-city traffic. As he crossed a street in the crosswalk with the green light in his favor, a driver going in the same direction failed to see him and turned right directly toward him. As the car approached him, John placed his hand on its hood, and vaulted himself out of the way.

He had gone about half a block when he stopped in his tracks, amazed at what had just happened. He had done the right thing so freely that he had hardly noticed it. He had not had a moment of fear. He had seen the threat, acted, and moved on. *How was this possible?*

Well, for a long time John had been practicing the Jesus Prayer, and he was praying attentively as he walked along the street. His focus was on the Lord, not on himself. So there was no fear. There was only right action. In retrospect, he realized that the only fear in the whole incident was the terror that appeared on the driver's face as John pushed himself out of harm's way.

Such focus on the Lord has another name. It is called faith. Looking at the Lord with our thoughts and our hearts keeps us open, alert, and confident. We begin to discover that the Lord will act in and through us in precisely the most appropriate way, even in the most unexpected circumstances. One experience like that and our faith in the Lord's loving presence bursts into fullness.

Let's look at the disciples and Jesus in regard to faith. We know they traveled around with Jesus because they loved him so much there was simply no alternative for them. They probably had some expectations, but they followed him for love.

That did not heal everything automatically, though. Experience had to come along with that initial love. Read Matthew 8:23-27. Notice that Jesus was not afraid at all; he was completely comfortable. When the disciples woke him up, he responded to them immediately, not to the danger first. He thought it was mighty strange for them to be so scared. He knew they had "little faith" and said so. Only then did he tend to the storm.

They were focused on the storm, the threat to themselves. In that moment, love him though they did, they were not focused on Jesus. Our focus makes a big difference in our attitude, both in a particular situation and in all of our life. If we focus on the frightening and thus feed our fear, we will be more and more scared, less and less aware of the Lord within his inner Kingdom in our heart.

In the midst of any situation, we can change our focus. In a workshop a few years ago, the group was invited to tackle fear by jumping off a high platform and catching a ring. The ring was not far, and besides, each participant was wearing a safety harness. One young woman had been habitually afraid of any heights, so she had difficulty just climbing to the platform. Once up there, she was paralyzed, she was so afraid. She stood and stood and stood there.

Finally, another member of the group shouted to her, "Make like Tarzan and GO!" It diverted her focus for just a moment. She pounded her chest, shouted "Me, Tarzan!" and leapt. Fear vanished. And, we learned later, her fear of heights never returned.

A simple shift of focus away from the storm and on to the Lord brought the results the disciples really wanted: their storm was calmed.

The Power of Faith to Heal

Another aspect of the power of faith is described in Mark 9:14-27. (See also Matthew 17:14-20.) The disciples had tried to do a special act of love: they wanted to heal an epileptic boy. They couldn't. Not enough power flowed through them.

Jesus is plain exasperated. Why don't the disciples have any faith? Then it turns out that the father, though he surely loves his son, isn't so sure about the healing either. Jesus says to him, "All things can be done for the one who believes." This belief is not a matter of subscribing to theological statements about God or Jesus; it is far deeper than that. It is a certainty that the desired result can occur (as we discussed in Chapter Four).

The boy's father is at least honest. His faith is half-baked, but he has some. He focuses on Jesus and asks for greater faith, that is, for more trusting certainty that the boy will be healed. It apparently happened within him. And I wonder if the father's inner healing that day wasn't actually more important than the new freedom of the son.

Jesus insists on the power of faith to heal. Healing is not always physical healing, of course. Many of us don't need physical healing; we all need healing of heart, healing of spirit. We need new foundations to be laid so we can move into the Kingdom.

We begin, as with most things, by clearing our thoughts so we know what we want. Do we want faith in the Lord, faith that trusts, faith that equals certainty? Do we want to love so much that fear is impossible? Or do we secretly relish our doubts and fears, dwelling on them often?

It is commonly assumed that no one clings to suffering, but that is not true. We do cling to our suffering, most often because our egocentric false self actually *likes* negative thoughts and emotions better than it likes positive thoughts and emotions.

Consider what "sells" on TV. The programming often emphasizes the negative—fears, problems, self-centered desires and passions, the determination to get one's own way, tensions. Do you doubt it? Observe the programs and commercials using this criterion: does this arouse negative or positive feelings? Consider what sells newspapers and magazines: negative emotion, scandal and terrors and horror stories. Someone likes these things—lots of someones!

Plenty of people choose the negatives in life; they like to complain, they like to find fault and criticize, they like to notice everything that is wrong in the world. What they seldom realize is that this attitude is itself the cause of their own unhappiness, their own sufferings.

We habitually feed our doubts and fears by focusing on negative things, awful possibilities. We spend much of our energy "building dungeons in the air," as John Galsworthy put it. These attitudes can be healed when we are willing to let go of them. Then we can focus on the Lord and ask for healing.

Increasing Faith and Trust

After we have asked the Lord to heal our negative attitudes and emotions, we can turn our attention to those things that increase faith and loving trustfulness.

What are they? There are hints in the stories you have just read. First, focus on the Lord, not on the threat. That will take an effort of will in the beginning. You may even, if you are attentive to yourself, notice that something in you actually resists this shift of focus.

Second, ask the Lord to increase your faith. Open your heart to him as wide as you are able. Be willing to be faith-filled. This is the beginning of deeper prayer.

Third, exercise your faith in small ways. Do not try to begin with moving mountains. Why? Because you will not believe; you will doubt on the basis of reason and the habitual way you interpret your experiences.

Read Matthew 21:18-22 and Luke 17:5-6. They are assertions more than instructions, but they give us a direction. Our faith needs to be purified from doubt and fear.

It is not so much whether we have a little or a lot of faith, Jesus says. A bit the size of a mustard seed is plenty. But it must be of a particular quality: doubt-free, fear-free, and purified of those negative inner states.

A seed is pure. It is only what it is and nothing else is mixed in with it. It "knows" what it is. That means it is able to lie in the ground, to take what it needs from the soil, to open its heart and push up into the light. It is even able to change its form, to become fully its own potential. That is the power of purity.

Last spring, for the first time ever, I bought gladiola bulbs. I didn't know a thing about them, but I examined them and then planted them in the ground. It took them so long to come up that I got curious and dug one up. It was sprouting all right, but it had a double task—I had planted them upside down! Nevertheless, they found their way. They came up and they blossomed. They were purely who they were, even when the new gardener didn't have a clue about what she was doing. That is the power of being pure, being only who we *truly* are.

We can be pure like a mustard seed. When we attain such purity, that is, when we are free of fear and doubt, we will be so full of trust and love and faith that in actuality nothing will be impossible for us. Life in the Kingdom will be ours.

So we do whatever we can to help ourselves become free of fear and doubt. We can do the thing we're afraid of. We can insist that the Lord knows what we don't know, that he has options we don't have, and we can then give him our concerns in an *act* of trust, even if our emotions are still not pure of fear or doubt. We must focus on his power and his love for us.

Then, gradually, faith and love will grow, fear and doubt will diminish. We come closer and closer to life in the Kingdom of certitude and love.

Reflection

1. Do you follow the Lord Jesus because you love him? because you are "supposed" to? because you were raised to go to church? Why do you "hang around" Jesus?
2. Muster your most honest determination to see clearly. Then ask yourself, Which of my negative attitudes do I secretly like? Which do I coddle and nurture and keep? Do I really want to keep doing this?
3. Try the following experiment for a week, keeping daily notes of your experience. Every time you find yourself thinking a negative thought, replace it deliberately with a positive thought—any positive thought. At the end of the week, ponder your experience. Then try it for another week and watch the gradual painless changes in your attitude. This is in reality the beginning of trust.

CHAPTER NINE

THE PASSION AND RESURRECTION: MODELS FOR TODAY

What jumps into your mind when you think of the Passion and Resurrection as models for today's experience of God's Kingdom? May I guess? Suffering. That is most people's common association with the last experiences of Jesus.

Christian tradition has always emphasized the power of suffering to draw us ever closer to God and keep us there. However, suffering and pain by itself will never do that. Everything depends on how we use the suffering that comes into our experience. If we don't know how to use it and turn it to the highest purposes, it is just misery and takes us nowhere. Reflection on the Passion and Resurrection of Jesus tells us a great deal about how to use our pain, about how not to waste our suffering.

We can begin by understanding that suffering is only useful when it displaces our egocentric self from its dominating position in our lives. The words and phrases that express this sublime process are not popular in our time: *yield, wait, accept, be grateful, endure, persist, request help, depend on God, love through all experiences, be peaceful, be calm.* The experiences represented by these and similar terms are not conducive to egocentricity. Self-centeredness tends to evaporate when we experience these qualities.

Words and phrases that express the opposite ideas and feelings (*strive, struggle, fight, insist, right now! do it myself*) tend to arouse selfish motives and to be driven by selfish intentions. If "me, mine, and keep" dominate life, the Kingdom is far away. Suffering itself can and sometimes does intensify selfishness, particularly when it is turned into self-pity (the greatest ego trip of them all). If we allow suffering to turn us only toward ourselves, that's where we get to stay. The Kingdom remains distant to our experience.

If we practice using suffering to teach us the qualities mentioned earlier, however, the sheer force behind our pain will grant us those qualities and transform us. We find ourselves living more and more in the Kingdom within ourselves, experiencing the reign of God in everyday discipleship.

Suffering itself, then, can be a practical tool, but its usefulness is not automatic. How we choose to use suffering is everything. That choice is always ours.

The Passion

How did Jesus use his suffering? What we wouldn't give for a personal description of what was going on inside Jesus during the hours of the Passion and Crucifixion! As it is, we have only the hints given in the gospels. You may want to refresh your memory about those events by reading Matthew 26:36 to 27:56, Mark 14:32 to 15:41, and Luke 22:39 to 23:43.

The principles we will recall by watching Jesus throughout the Passion are useful for making suffering transformative. Even more important, they are principles of living in the Kingdom, of being Jesus' faithful disciple. They are applicable to all of our life experiences. It was only because Jesus had lived by these principles all his life that he was actually able to do so under extremely painful conditions.

It is said that stress reveals what we truly are like. If so, the stress of the Passion revealed a strong, centered Jesus who lived only for God and for other people. Here is some of the evidence and it gives us direction for using suffering.

First, Jesus asked God for help. In the Garden and on the cross, he cried out to his beloved Father to help him. And he received help, didn't he? It is described in the paragraphs on the Agony in the Garden. On the cross, Jesus begins to quote Psalm 22, which begins in lament and ends in a strong affirmation of praise and confidence in God (you may wish to reread it). We can surmise that the help Jesus received at this moment on the cross was deeply interior and totally strengthening.

We, too, not only in pain but all the time and in everything, will ask for God's help if we want to live in the Kingdom. For every project, every task, every hope and dream, as well as every pain, we can ask for God's help. It is always given. We can count on it if our hearts are open. It's a fact of good discipleship, an experience of the Kingdom within.

Jesus surrendered to what was coming and to what happened to him all the way through his suffering. He had always surrendered to the small and the great directions of the Father within. Now he faced a cruel death—and surrendered to it for love of his Father. He surrendered to all the physical pains of the Passion and Crucifixion. We do not see him squirming or resisting. He surrendered also to the mockeries and psychological onslaughts of the whole experience. He did not defend himself. He did not resist. His teachings had been the same: turn the other cheek, do not resist when evil happens to you, go the extra mile.

Jesus had been accused of many things, many times. He answered his accusers calmly and without vindictiveness. So now, in extremity, he lived as he always had. It is a perfect illustration of a Kingdom principle: surrender to God and to all circumstances, both little and huge, for the love of God.

When we understand this idea, something in us immediately begins to resist and argue, doesn't it? In me as well as in you, that which resists is our ego-centeredness. Eventually, it will have to die as completely as Jesus died on the cross. In the meantime, we can practice by surrendering our own way to the circumstances we have, to discover in them how to love God.

Here is one simple (but not always easy) possibility for doing that: when you are accused of something, don't flare up with self-defense. Clamp your mouth shut. Wait a little. (On this point, I am still teaching myself!)

In that pause, stop thinking up excuses and justifications. You don't really need to answer. Inside, you can simply let yourself feel the fire for a bit. It won't kill the real you. It will surely help displace the ego. It is a prelude to transformation.

Then, if there is an issue that needs to be discussed, you can discuss it as calmly as Jesus answered his accusers and as definitely as Jesus ignored his mockers. Turn to God inside and thank him for this opportunity to learn surrender.

Jesus had to accept his pain almost all alone, except for the presence of God. Human support was not given to him in his last twenty-four hours amid the horrors. Jesus accepted that. He accepted the fact that he, like all other people, had lived and would die largely alone. Sometimes when challenging events occur, we want to run for help. Before we run for human help, we should run to God. Human help is wonderful too. But if we need to learn a lesson on our own, people may not be there to support us. To learn self-reliance in this way is a good thing. It strengthens us and it strengthens our dependence on God as well. Healthy self-reliance on God, based on surrender to the reality of sometimes being humanly alone, is a Kingdom quality.

Throughout the Passion, Jesus spoke only as much as was genuinely necessary. That was very little, wasn't it? If we take him here, too, as our example, what do we learn?

We talk too much! Remember the last time you had beloved houseguests, how you talked and talked, trying to "catch up" with each others' lives? After hours of talk, what happened to your energy?

We talk too much, and it throws our energy to the winds. We talk too much, and it gives us noisy minds. We talk too much, and it closes off inner perceptions. It is a constant "hype" and one that is not easy to come away from.

In times of suffering, we need our energy. Pain demands energy. If we talk away our precious inner resources, prayer will be more difficult and surrender will be nearly impossible.

On a thirty-day silent retreat I made some years ago, conversation was nonexistent. Spiritual direction and one afternoon each week for sharing were the only times we talked. Energy abounded. Prayer deepened. Sensitivity to ourselves and one another expanded. It was amazing how much we gained interiorly by talking much less.

Daily life requires conversation. We like to share, and our love is enhanced by true communication. But also—we talk too much and deprive ourselves of vitality by doing it. We need our vitality for daily life and especially for life in the Kingdom. Kingdom life gives life; it also requires energy for full participation. Let's practice Jesus' example and not dissipate energy unnecessarily in unnecessary talk.

As we have already seen, Jesus forgave his torturers. Right in the middle of the terrible pain they had caused, he forgave them. Pain, though unjust, did not deter his love. Let's not let suffering lure us into holding on to anger. Rather, let's *use* the pain and forgive those who inflict it. Then our own Kingdom benefits will double!

Through the Passion, as through his life, Jesus reached out to those around him to help them. He offered comforting words, perhaps met the eyes of others to give love. From the cross, he welcomed the "Good Thief" into Paradise. He ignored no one, even accepting the help given by Simon Cyrene. That acceptance itself was a gift to Simon, wasn't it?

Sometimes difficulties make us temporarily unaware of others' sufferings—or just others' presence, their lives, themselves. If we allow anything in our experience to turn our awareness aside from others, we limit our participation in the Kingdom of Christ. We forget, in those moments, that we are disciples.

We may want to ask ourselves, then, whether we want to remain so fascinated by our own suffering. If not, we turn our attention in love to someone else and try to help them a little. Notice what happens when you do this—it may be quite a revelation! We can practice focusing on others, even in difficulties. One place to make the effort is a doctor's or dentist's waiting room.

I saw this very thing once while I waited for a doctor's appointment. A woman in poor clothing, looking quite harried, went to the receptionist's window to explain why she was so far behind on her doctor bill. The receptionist was sympathetic but insisted that at least ten dollars had to be paid before the woman could receive any more treatment. The woman turned and left.

Then a woman who had been waiting to see the doctor went to the window and gave the startled receptionist ten dollars for the first woman's payment. She asked to remain anonymous and instructed the receptionist to go get the poor woman and put her on the appointment schedule. When the giver turned back to sit down, I saw that her faced was marked with "target points" for radiation; she herself was seriously ill, perhaps with cancer. It was a moment of Kingdom awareness.

At the end of his Passion, Jesus gave himself to God in death, just as he had given himself to God every day of his life. Can't we practice the same thing? Give the day to God, give the task to God, give the pain to God, but always remember to give yourself to God every single day. Then, when death arrives—as it definitely will—you can give yourself to God in that moment as well.

What will happen next? What happened next to Jesus?

The Resurrection

Once again, we may wish that Jesus could tell us what the Resurrection was like. We can barely imagine, for we don't yet know what death is like. What we can know, if we let it into our hearts, is that surrender to all little deaths leads to life.

Our practice deaths may not involve physical death for a long time. We may lose something or someone. We may burn away the power of our ego—decidedly a death. We may be injured. All kinds of circumstances may taste like a small death.

The most important death for Kingdom life is the death of self-centeredness. When the Lord alone is the center of our attention, our love, our efforts, and our hope, then we have experienced the death of the false, or small, self. It is extraordinarily difficult to allow this to happen, but when someone manages to let the little self die, the brilliant glory of full Kingdom life emerges from the corpse.

Resurrection surely had a perceivable dimension, for Jesus'

disciples did finally learn to recognize him and respond to him. He was different, though, and none of them knew him at first. He was glory. A different kind of inner perception probably was required to relate to the resurrected Jesus. But the disciples learned it, and the ones who learned it the quickest were those whose self-centeredness had most nearly died. Mary Magdalene was the first.

The Resurrection is the fulfillment of the Kingdom within. It suffuses everything, permeates one's whole being, transforms the person completely from the inside out. It's been coming all along. The way of discipleship has given many intimations of resurrection.

Every little death we have endured and not wasted has given us a taste of new life, unexpected understanding, fresh joyfulness, deeper inner riches. Resurrection is the promise of death. New life is the fullness of the Kingdom.

That means that while life in the Kingdom, as you now know, can be experienced in this life with more and more intensity and beauty, it just keeps on going through and after our physical death. The Kingdom within is the one thing we *can* take with us!

Reflection

1. What is your habitual attitude when suffering or pain occurs in your life? Do you resist with all your might? Do you yield to the situation? Where is your focus during suffering?
2. How self-defensive are you? This is very subtle, and learning to let it go will take a long time. Be patient with yourself. But begin with what you can see in yourself. When you find yourself in a defensive position, PAUSE. Follow the suggestions in this chapter. You can leave this habit far behind!

3. How much talk is too much? As you speak and before you speak again, ask yourself: Is this necessary talk? does it contribute to a valued relationship? is it kind? is it gossip about others (even so-called positive gossip)? Pray about this subject, asking for your awareness to increase. Write down your self-observations and discoveries.

CONCLUSION

One of the two or three most familiar parables about the Kingdom and the meaning of discipleship is the story of the Prodigal Son, sometimes called the Lost Son. You will find it in Luke 15:11-32.

The interpretation celebrates the steadfast love of the father in the parable. He is there for his sons. He stays with both of them in constant love—for the "good" son who stays home and for the "not-so-good" son who wanders far away. This love of God for all his children is the axis around which everything in the Kingdom really revolves. Without that, there is nothing—nothing at all.

So here at the end of our exploration of the Kingdom, we can reiterate the one thing we know for sure: God is for us, no matter what. As Jesus said, "...it is your Father's good pleasure to give you the kingdom" (Luke 12:32).

We understand the symbolism of the father in the parable. Who is the lost son, however? Is he the one who actually lives a degenerate life, who commits terrible sins, who throws away his life in debauchery? Too often, we have thought so.

Now let's look deeper. While that interpretation may help us appreciate God's love for all, it lets us avoid the more profound significance of the parable. For when spirituality, one's relationship with God, is the question, then the "lost son" is you, is me. He is all of us.

All of us have, to some extent, taken the gifts of the good God and thrown them away. All of us have wandered far from the Lord. Our own sense of God's being distant from us testifies to our inner wanderings. The situation of the lost son is our inner situation. Like him, we must "come to our senses" and return home.

That is what we are doing when we seek the Kingdom, when we begin to realize that the only effort of total and pure worth in this life is finding the Kingdom of God within our own hearts. Everything else good is a reflection of this Kingdom. Now we want to know God directly; we want to be God's in actuality now and forever.

So we head homeward; and as we go, we become more and more acutely aware of the ways we have missed the mark through the years. We have been ignorant. We have done wrong things, as everyone has. We have wasted many opportunities. We could go on like that for a long time—and some of us do.

The long walk back, so to speak, may not be easy. Our souls reproach us. But because we know what kind of reception we can expect, the stones along the way will not hurt our feet so much. We know something the lost son in the story didn't know: we know we will be totally welcome when we arrive. God will receive us with love, celebrate our return, honor us, and reinstate us in his heart and his life—and now become our life as well. It is life in the Kingdom, where we dwell together with God in endless joy. The Kingdom is there—or rather, here—for us now. It will be where we are forever.

The loving Father rejoices over every one of us who comes homeward toward the Kingdom. For those who do not come home, another response appears in God's compassion. Jesus experienced it too. In Matthew 23:37-38, Jesus laments over Jerusalem. It was a city he loved well, as all Jews did. Moreover, he loved its people more than they even guessed. He mourns over them because he wanted them to come to his love to be protected and cared for—but they would not come. Because they would not, suffering came.

Jesus' sadness is for all those who do not want to come home to the Kingdom, for whatever reason. He is sad because they are ignoring the greatest good in life but also because self-imposed isolation from the Lord brings increased suffering. It is a suffering that cannot be mitigated until the person in pain makes that all-important turn to face homeward and begins to walk.

On the other hand, just as the father of the lost son rejoiced in his return, Jesus told of the Lord's rejoicing over the finding and return of all lost sheep. Matthew 18:10-14 and Luke 15:1-7 give us this lasting image. Not only does the Lord rejoice when someone is recovered, he is active in seeking out the ones who are lost.

Combining the insights of the two stories, we can say that we lost ones must acknowledge that we are lost and turn our hearts in God's direction. Simultaneously, God, who always knows where we are, will help us make the journey back home, carrying us on his shoulders if need be and rejoicing all the way.

The only question remaining for us, then, is this all-important one: Will the Lord rejoice over us as over a found one? Or will he lament over us as over unwilling Jerusalem?

It's up to us.

Don't miss...

Discovering the Spirit of the Gospels, Volume II: John
Formerly titled *Witness to the Light*, this is the companion volume to *Discovering the Spirit of the Gospels, Volume I*. Together these two volumes provide a treasure–trove of spiritually enriching insights into the gospels. *$4.95*

More on Scripture from Marilyn Gustin...

How to Read and Pray the Passion Story
Invites you to study the Scriptural portrayal of Jesus during his passion and crucifixion through the Synoptic Gospels. Also includes discussion of how John's Gospel differs from the Synoptics and offers you ways to reflect and pray on the passion in order to deepen your capacity to receive the grace of Christ. *$4.95*

How to Read and Pray the Christmas Story
Explores the birth stories written by Matthew and Luke, and reflects on John's Prologue along with examining the characters, symbols, and associations in Scripture to offer you a way to deepen your relationship with Christ through the Christmas story. *$3.95*

How to Read and Pray the Parables
Emphasizes the practical meaning of Jesus' parables to help you gain a spiritual perspective for everyday life. *$2.50*

Also available from Marilyn Gustin...

Twelve Bible–based audios on everyday concerns
Each of these informative pamphlets cite appropriate Scripture passages that are related to very specific areas of daily life. If you want to start living your life more closely with God but aren't sure where to begin, this series can help you get started. *$9.95 each*

What the Bible Says About...

Community	Money and Possessions
Confidence	Peace of Mind
Discipline	The Power of Speech
Forgiveness	Prayer
Friendship	Suffering
Generosity	Trust

Also available in pamphlet form *$1 each*

Order from your local bookstore or write
Liguori Publications
Box 060, Liguori, MO 63057-9999
(Please add $1 * for postage and handling to orders under $5; $1.50 for orders between $5 and $15; $2 for orders over $15.)
* For single-pamphlet order, send $1 plus stamped, self-addressed envelope.